The Future of Foundations

Some Reconsiderations

Change Magazine Press

Part 2 of this book has also been published in the 1976-77 annual report of the Russell Sage Foundation and is reprinted here by permission. Copyright © 1978 by the Russell Sage Foundation.

The Future of Foundations:
Some Reconsiderations
Addition for Chapter 2
Footnotes

1. John Stuart Mill, *Principles of Political Economy*, edited by J. M. Robson (University of Toronto Press, 1965), Chap. XI, para. 16.

2. Marion R. Fremont-Smith, *Foundations and Government* (New York: Russell Sage Foundation, 1965).

3. Waldemar A. Nielsen, *The Big Foundations* (New York: Columbia University Press, 1972), p. 309.

4. Walter Trattner, *From Poor Law to Welfare State* (New York: The Free Press, 1974).

5. Edith Fisch, Doris Free, and Esther Schater, *Charities and Charitable Foundations* (Pomona, N.Y.: Lord Publications, 1975), pp. 58-62.

6. Reproduced in *Legal Instruments of Foundations*, compiled by F. Emerson Andrews (New York: Russell Sage Foundation, 1958).

7. John M. Glenn, Lilian Brandt, and F. Emerson Andrews, *Russell Sage Foundation 1907-1946* (New York: Russell Sage Foundation, 1947), p. 5.

8. Waldemar Nielsen, p. 34.

9. Quoted by Thomas Parrish in "The Foundations: A Special American Institution," in *The Future of Foundations*, edited by Fritz Heimann (Englewood Cliffs, N.J.: Prentice-Hall, 1973), p. 14.

10. Robert H. Brenner, "Private Philanthropy and Public Needs: Historical Perspective," *Research Papers*, Vol. I (sponsored by the Commission on Private Philanthropy and Public Needs, Washington, D.C.: Department of the Treasury, 1977), pp. 89-114.

11. If the purposes of a charitable trust cannot be fulfilled, the trustees or the charity commissioners may apply to the courts to rearrange the terms of the trust to enable the funds to be applied in a way which they think is nearest (cy pres) to what the donor would have intended.

12. Waldemar Nielsen, p. 384.

13. Franklin D. Roosevelt provided a foreword to a Russell Sage publication in 1935 on regional planning, "Outline of Town and City Planning: A Review of Past Efforts With Modern Aims," in which he described city planning as "among the most important needs of our modern civilization." His interest in the subject had been fostered by his uncle, Frederic A. Delano, who had been chairman of the Committee on the Regional Plan for New York.

14. Waldemar Nielsen, p. 382.

15. Ben Whitaker, *The Philanthropoids* (New York: William Morrow, 1974), p. 170.

16. Ida C. Merriam and Alfred M. Skolnik, *Social Welfare Expenditures Under Public Programs 1929-66* (Washington, D.C.: Department of HEW, Social Security Administration, Office of Records and Statistics, Report No. 25, 1968), Table III.

17. *Ibid.*, Table I.

18. Source: Frank Dickinson, *The Changing Place of Philanthropy in the American Economy* (New York: Columbia University Press for the National Bureau of Economic Research, 1970). Appendix I uses a somewhat different and longer series but the substantive point remains the same.

19. Keynote address, Twenty-seventh Annual Conference of Council on Foundations, May 1976.

20. Martin L. Landau, "Redundancy, Rationality, and the Problem of Duplication Overlap," *Public Administration Review* 29 (July-August, 1969), p. 356.

21. An example is the side effects of parents' fund-raising activities (bake sales and the like). These activities were primarily designed to raise funds for their children's school, but the side effect was to involve parents in the school. Title I compensatory education funds can substitute for the money produced in this way, but it is then necessary to stimulate the formation of organizations such as parents' advisory committees to try to substitute more or less successfully for the side effects that have been lost. We thank Frank Levy for the example.

Contents

1

2

3

Contributors

Landrum R. Bolling is chairman and chief executive officer of the Council on Foundations and a former president of the Lilly Endowment.

George W. Bonham is executive director of the Council on Learning and editor-in-chief of *Change* Magazine.

McGeorge Bundy, who was Special Assistant for National Security Affairs to John F. Kennedy, has been president of the Ford Foundation since 1966.

James A. Douglas has been studying the voluntary nonprofit sector since 1977, first at the Russell Sage Foundation and currently at Yale University's Institution for Social and Policy Studies.

Fred M. Hechinger is president of the New York Times Company Foundation and special advisor to the newspaper's publisher, as well as a contributing editor to *Saturday Review*.

John H. Knowles has been president of the Rockefeller Foundation since 1972 and is a former general director of Massachusetts General Hospital.

Waldemar A. Nielsen is president of a consulting group on corporate social policy and a fellow of the Aspen Institute for Humanistic Studies.

B.J. Stiles is one of three deputy chairmen of the National Endowment for the Humanities and acting director of its Division of State Programs.

Aaron Wildavsky is a professor of political science on leave from the University of California, Berkeley, and was president of the Russell Sage Foundation in 1977-78.

Paul N. Ylvisaker is dean of the faculty and Charles William Eliot Professor of Education at the Graduate School of Education of Harvard University. He is the author of *Private Philanthropy and Public Affairs*, published by the Commission on Private Philanthropy and Public Needs.

1

Some Basic Questions

George W. Bonham

American philanthropy, especially the large and what are here referred to as the "knowledgeable" foundations, has in recent decades significantly contributed to a proud history of rich cultural and social imagination. Without these foundations' encouragement and moneys, many of our national ambitions of a higher order might never have been realized. But there is now growing doubt that such foundation achievements can be sustained in the future. If they cannot, it will prove a great loss to the country and to our central democratic tradition of voluntarism. Nonetheless, facts must be faced, and capabilities and weaknesses enumerated and reckoned with. Unhappily, perhaps, foundations have been more accepting of praise than of criticism, a stonewalling mentality that has contributed to their present difficulties.

It is all too easy to cite the foundations' current inadequacies without also reminding ourselves of their enormous accomplishments. Their great deeds began as early as the twenties, when they helped provide educational opportunities for the nation's black leadership. Foundations early on anticipated the complex dilemmas of world population growth, the problems of race, the crises of the public schools, the depressed state of faculty salaries, the endangered future of public broadcasting, and the loss of direction in American higher education in the wake of the apoplectic sixties. Gunnar Myrdal, James Conant, and Clark Kerr made their profound impact with the vast resources of imaginative foundations behind them, and their work is only part of an eloquent record of solid human progress.

But it is the expectation born of this impressive record of social invention and anticipation of human need that may be the foundations' present undoing. Like most other modern institutions, the foundations have now been overtaken by events that are largely not of their making, events which most philanthropies are equipped to address only marginally. Not even the federal budget is capable of cashiering any but the most basic problem areas of an entitlement-laden society.

The trouble with foundations is thus the trouble with most other public welfare institutions. And if they are singled out as targets of special criticism, it is perhaps in fact because much is still expected of them. The foundations' idealistic rhetoric sometimes exceeds the true possibilities within their grasp, and there are always public penalties to be assessed when such gaps between promise and results are so widely perceived. But whatever one's appetite for social change, it is beyond the ability of most human enterprises to control it, let alone get ahead of it. Any careful study of performance in this regard shows ample evidence that foundations in particular are among the least likely modern institutions to support and encourage social change with any demonstrable conviction and continuity. Incrementalism is their more favored course of action.

Even the most socially sophisticated foundations now find themselves facing a widening breach between their expressed hopes for a higher social order and their abilities to move matters in more than circumscribed ways. "If there is an evident lesson to be learned from the turbulence of the times in which we live," wrote Carnegie's President Alan Pifer 10 years ago, "it is that the nation has no higher requirement today than a flexible capacity for rapid change in its social institutions. In the light of this national imperative, every agency which can serve the common good by facilitating the processes of institutional change toward a more just, healthier, better educated, and more universally prosperous national and world society has a very special value, and perhaps none more so than foundations." While this approach to solving human dilemmas is to be admired, it is nevertheless true that no significant American foundation is now capable of seriously matching its programs with such high social ambitions.

In recent years, the foundation world has become somewhat more self-critical and somewhat less self-righteous, but almost always as an isolated response to the threat of governmental intervention. While it has concerned itself in the main with filling the breaches occasioned by tax and regulatory challenges, it has as a field rarely made a concerted attempt to analyze its sense of mission and future prospects. It displays a curious mentality, especially since it enjoys an inherent capability to engage in rational analysis of major social issues, at least outside of itself.

The case for an internal reconsideration of foundation functions has not been helped by the sometimes irrational attacks on philanthropy from both the right and the left. Ideology aside, there are always the folk suspicions and hostilities shown toward those holding the money bags at the counting tills. Nonetheless, the erosion of public confidence in the foundations may well be matched by an equal erosion of competence *inside* the foundations. There are disquieting symptoms. By their genesis and source of power, foundations retain the predominantly conservative views one might expect to find reflected in the ideological temper of an erstwhile plutocracy. Foundations, with few exceptions, are philanthropic extensions of the banks, the securities market, and America's business leadership, and they act accordingly. This tendency toward sticking to the center, if not to the right, is frequently further reinforced by the foundation professionals themselves, who are usually former academics. Thus rigidities of political philosophy from the top conspire with intellectual rigidities from the staff below. It is a condition that is hardly likely to nurture the new shapers of the world.

Such inherent conservatism produces, of course, a useful organizational base for the prudent dispensing of funds, but it is rarely the breeding ground for the risk-taking endeavors frequently suggested in foundations' annual reports. From the evidence at hand, the social risks foundations are likely to take have been comparatively small. Such risks are much admired in official philanthropic documents but are in fact avoided like the plague by foundation staffs with the plea that they lie "beyond their program area."

If this is not then the golden age of foundations, the question must be raised as to whether the impact of their contributions on American life is now diminishing to a point of no return. The potential for continued national service remains, but the foundations work under serious constraints that will make their life more difficult in the future. Whether any national institution that by definition must make meritocratic decisions can for long survive our current penchant for egalitarianism is an open question. The debate over whether this country can be both excellent and equal remains as unresolved today as when John Gardner launched it nearly 20 years ago. It would surely be in the interests of much that is best about this country if foundations could continue to play a fruitful role in social leadership and human progress.

But whether they have the inherent foresight and organizational strength to do so in the future is quite another matter. Even among the leading foundations, performance varies to a degree that must surely be worrisome even to the most loyal philanthropic supporters. In foundation work at least, size of endowment is no guarantee of competence. There is simply more incompetence in foundation work than one wishes to imagine. Brilliance is sometimes matched by mediocrity, made more tolerable by the ameliorating capacity to give out money.

There are still other problems. In the process of "professionalizing" foundations, staffs have grown top-heavy and excessively bureaucratic. A foundation that dispenses $10 million a year may now require a professional staff of 20, when it took half that number 20 years ago. And there is no evidence to show that moneys are being given away more wisely because of such multiplying staffs. There is increasing evidence to the contrary that the often labyrinthine ways of foundation processes now seriously impede, rather than enhance, bold and imaginative policies.

There is a certain irony in all of this, since foundations are fond of regarding themselves as countervailing forces to the heavy hand of government. But some are now as enthralled with administrative paperwork as their governmental counterparts, and in some cases more so. As one of our most prominent social observers recently put it, the foundations are rapidly turning themselves into "mini-HEWs." It is an unhappy comparison, but nonetheless an accurate one. Some foundations have carried the governmental model even further by demanding evaluative procedures and performance reviews that give them in effect operating control over the work of their grantees. It is a temptation that has not yet reached calamitous proportions, but represents a dangerous precedent that seems to be taking hold.

In many foundations, especially those that are corporate and family dominated, major funding decisions are often made not by the professional staffs but by executive fiat. Such personal dominance in the philanthropic decision-making process not only raises serious questions but also quickly results in the demoralization of the professional staff. Either way, such practices are undesirable in foundation life today.

No recitation of current problem areas would be complete without noting the growing trend of some professional foundation staffs to represent within their own foundations special interest groups. Such internal sponsorship can result in staff struggles for a larger share of the limited foundation budget pie, which in time must surely prove damaging to the organization as a whole. In protecting one's program turf to the exclusion of adjacent philanthropic interests, organizational myopia, rather than enlightened vision, is the usual outcome.

Since these are not the halcyon days for even the major foundations, prospects for finding professional satisfaction within them are now less likely as well. In this respect, at least, both the American academy and philanthropy suffer increasingly from tired blood, from a psychology of operating out of the trenches, and from a growing inability to attract the best people, as they once did. The best and the brightest are no longer seeking foundation careers, except perhaps as a way station. Treading water, rather than making waves, is now the general rule. Ground is still broken, to be sure. But it is familiar ground, and more often than not it has been tilled many times before.

Where does one go from here? For the academic profession, for which many of these same diagnoses apply, the continued health of philanthropy represents an essential requisite for the viability of its own future. For quite understandable reasons, scholars can hardly be expected to act as philanthropy's most evenhanded critics. Incestuousness rarely produces scholarly critics who can be both fair-minded and independent of spirit. Nonetheless, academics should show more concern and interest for philanthropy's welfare than they now seem capable of. Both fields need each other's continued vigor, and the loss of either would represent a calamity soon to be regretted.

The contributors to these pages make no effort to develop a

blueprint for the foundations' future. No such blueprint does in fact exist. There are 10,000 foundations, with 10,000 different futures. But what can be gleaned from these pages is a mode of thought, a discussion of concerns, that makes interesting reading for anyone concerned with the future of foundations. The opinions expressed here are little more than a snapshot of one moment in time. But if this book encourages other more precise observations about the state of philanthropy, it will have been worth the efforts of the contributors.

The discussion (beginning on page 44) of a group of knowledgeable people—both foundation executives and foundation watchers—was occasioned by an opportunity to elaborate and critique a paper by James Douglas and Aaron Wildavsky on the future of foundations. Their view is one that neither the two authors nor our commentators expected could garner wholehearted endorsement. But it served as a useful framework for discussion. What it ultimately teaches us about these deliberations on the philanthropic future is that the foundation world is made up of some highly intelligent professionals, though they are far from unanimous about what the ultimate usefulness of their work is likely to be.

The late John D. Rockefeller 3rd, speaking a year ago about the third sector, of which the foundation world is an integral part, warned that "if we allow the third sector to continue to erode, we will wake up some morning to find that we are living in a very different society. And if we ever have a two-sector system, then the trend toward one sector will have begun. I do not believe that the American people would consciously choose this path. It must not happen by default."

Whether Mr. Rockefeller's fears will come to pass depends not only on a fuller public understanding of the foundations' role in a changing world but also on their abilities to face up to their inherent handicaps of limited imagination and an increasingly arthritic structure. They cannot rest on the laurels of past deeds, nor can they allow themselves to believe that doling out money is any more sufficient justification for their existence. Unhappily for the foundations, perhaps, that very act now entails special obligations, not special privileges.

2

The Knowledgeable Foundations

James Douglas and Aaron Wildavsky

The age of optimism in public policy is passing, and a time of skepticism is upon us. As a nation, we are sadly aware of our collective incapacity to do good at will. The question is arising whether we would not be wiser in using what we have learned— negative knowledge is not to be despised; "do no harm" is not the worst of adages—not as an excuse for abandoning hope, but rather to strengthen our resolve to perfect what Herbert Croly rightly called the "promise of American life."

In the midst of this effusion of self-doubt, what will become of the characteristically American foundation, with its quintessential optimism about our ability to right wrongs, based on a fundamental understanding of human behavior? Foundations cannot be understood apart from their associates and their rivals. The flowering of foundations before World War I, their surge of new life after World War II, and their malaise at the bicentennial are all explicable in terms of the relationship of their resources and aspirations to the institutions of learning, upon which they depend for knowledge, and to government, upon whose tacit goodwill they must rely. Understanding is important; grasping the evolution of foundations helps to explain their present plight. But the promise of understanding should be dignified by the performance of action—a heightened conception of the positive role of foundations in new times.

In a classic statement of the liberal view of what Jeremy Bentham had called the "agenda of government," John Stuart Mill wrote, "There is scarcely anything really important to the general interest, which it may not be desirable or even necessary that the government should take on itself, not because private individuals cannot effectively perform it, but because they will not.... In these cases, the mode in which the government can surely demonstrate the sincerity with which it intends the greatest good of its subjects is by doing the things which are made incumbent on it by the helplessness of the public, in such a manner as shall tend not to increase and perpetuate, but to correct that helplessness."[1] Foundations, in the past, reversed this process, seeking to do "anything really important to the general interest," which government "will not perform" and doing it "in such a manner as shall tend not to perpetuate" their own activity but rather in order to encourage government to take over the responsibility. Foundations cannot continue in this manner when government has shown its willingness to embark upon almost any field of philanthropic activity and has thereby preempted the traditional fields of foundation activity. But foundations may yet find their role in doing those things that government "cannot effectively perform," or at least those things that can be undertaken more effectively by an independent body.

In the Beginning

The Foundation is a very ancient form of institution. Marion Fremont-Smith traces its origins back to ancient Egypt and Chaldea and shows an almost continuous development since the Roman law of the first century B.C.[2] Even today, in the field of medicine, in many forms of social work, and perhaps above all in institutions of higher learning, many institutions still exist in Western Europe that were established as private foundations centuries ago.

Lest we be misled by an accidental similarity of terminology, we need to be clear that the medieval foundations were indeed similar to the modern foundation. In essence, they were. Essentially, a foundation is a private institution which disposes of private funds for a public purpose. The medieval foundations, like the modern ones, were established by a free gift of their original founders from their own resources. The direction of the institution was, and still is in some real way, independent of the public authorities, although it is (and always has been) subject to some measure of public control. The public authorities may impose constraints under which private foundations must operate, but, by definition, there must be enough room for foundations to choose for themselves what they do and how they do it for the term "private" to remain applicable to them. Once the government constraints become so tight that this freedom disappears, it becomes meaningless to speak of these institutions still as private foundations and more accurate to say that they have been taken over by the state. Of course, this can, and quite often does, happen. In England, for example, many grammar schools originally established as private foundations became absorbed into the public education system.

Modern foundations often seem chary of the adjective "private." Yet it describes an essential characteristic of the institution. It is perfectly true that foundations receive special privileges, such as tax relief, from the public authority. They have done so from time immemorial; and how far in return the public authorities may impose restrictions or seek to control their activities has been the subject of debate for centuries. As early as the time of the Magna Carta, feudal lords were objecting that lands granted to charitable foundations did not have to pay the feudal dues that would otherwise have been owed in respect of their tenure. Given that land was, at the time, the principal form of asset with which a foundation could be endowed, the exemption from feudal dues was not all that different from the tax exemption which the income from the endowments of a modern foundation enjoys. It is also true that, other things being equal (which they rarely are) the tax exemption for foundation moneys represents a loss in revenue and increases the amount of taxation that would otherwise need to be raised from other taxpayers. However, this does not give public officials the right to tell foundations what to do with their money. Money that is raised from taxation passes into the public domain, and every modern state places upon public officials, answerable directly or indirectly through the mechanism of the ballot box to the taxyers, the responsibility for deciding how public money should be allocated. Money that is exempt from taxation, however, has never passed into the public domain, and its allocation does not therefore become the responsibility of elected representatives. The distinction may seem a fine one, but it is essential to the independence of foundations, which in turn is what enables them to be an alternative to, as opposed to part of, the administrative processes of government.

Waldemar Nielsen argues that foundations, more than most major national institutions, are "inner directed." "They are not subject to the stimulus and discipline of the customers, stockholders, voters, or student bodies. Nor does government regulation, although more intrusive than in the past, do much more than mark off broad boundaries within which foundations are free to operate. What they are, therefore, and what they do is essentially determined by the controlling forces within them."[3] It is this ability to decide their own goals and allocate their own resources, according to their own internal system of administration, that distinguishes foundations from an arm of government. If this distinction were to be lost and foundation money treated as public money by virtue of its tax-exempt status, it is difficult to see on what constitutional principle foundations could resist the claims of elected representatives of the people to decide their priorities and determine their programs.

Of course, public authorities, when they are granting special privileges such as tax exemptions, are entitled to impose such conditions as they see fit upon individuals or organizations that voluntarily choose to avail themselves of the privileges. Essentially, the condition in the case of foundations is that the funds exempted from taxation be committed to the service of the public good. This broad principle is further fleshed out in detailed prohibitions against "self-dealing," against "attempting to influence legislation," against "intervention in political campaigns for public office," and certain other specific activities. The detailed provisions have varied at different periods of history, as has the rigor of the control imposed by authorities, but the principle of exerting some form of public control upon private foundations is ancient, and the 800 years or so of debate surrounding the laws of mortmain are testimony to the perennial debate between private foundations and national legislatures. The fact that the word "mortmain" means "dead hand" suggests that the rhetoric of the opponents of foundations has not changed greatly in 800 years.

A good deal of ingenuity and subtle psychology has been devoted to distinguishing the objectives of the medieval founders from those of more recent times. Yet the distinction is probably more apparent than real. William of Wykeham may have spoken of his hopes of eternal salvation and the glory of the Blessed Virgin, but he was also a public official, temporarily in disgrace, who was well aware that a country ravaged by war and the aftereffects of the Black Death needed the educated administrators (both in state and church) which his foundations were to provide. It is rather striking that, 600 years later, his foundations are still providing both the British civil service and the Church of England with recruits who have very much the same qualities, although one must admit that there were times in the intervening years when the founder's intentions were not very well represented.

One distinction between medieval foundations and those established after the Reformation is in the constitution of the body established. Typically, in a medieval foundation, the assets were vested in the master and fellows of the college or hospital, and this body was, and remains, the governing body of the institution. The model for this appears to have been derived from monastic prototypes, in which the master was analogous to the abbot, the fellows to the chapter, and the institution's statutes analogous to the rule. After the Reformation, foundations more typically were set up as charitable trusts, with the assets vested in a separate board of trustees. In the medieval model, trustees, staff, and even the beneficiaries, or "donees," were often the same people. It may well be that today, when we hear a great deal about participation, student power, and faculty government, the time has come to look afresh at the medieval collegiate pattern, with its corollaries of collective responsibility and, formally at least, decisions made by consensus.

The early American foundations did not differ greatly from the charities established at the same period in Europe. They consisted of schools and universities—such as Harvard and Yale—hospitals and medical schools, missionary societies, libraries—such as that founded by Benjamin Franklin in 1731—parks, almshouses, orphanages, organizations "to assist widows and orphans, immigrants and Negroes, debtors and prisoners, aged females and young prostitutes; to supply the poor with food, fuel, medicine, and employment; to promote morality, thrift, industrious habits; to educate poor children; to reform gamblers, drunkards, and juvenile delinquents."[4] Comic examples notwithstanding, they all had a specific purpose, and they operated fairly directly on what their founders saw as qualifying as a social ill or a public need.

Toward the end of the nineteenth century, and in the early years of the twentieth, two developments became apparent. The first was the attempt to get to the root causes of particular social problems. Edith Fisch, *et al.*, write, "The foundation created by George Peabody in 1867 is regarded as the prototype of the modern foundation in that its broad purposes are aimed at the discovery and prevention of social ills rather than at their amelioration."[5] The second development was a greater broadening in the stated purposes for which foundations are established. The purpose of the Carnegie Corporation, created in 1911, was, according to its articles of incorporation, "the advancement and diffusion of knowledge and understanding" among the people of the United States and the British dominions and colonies. The charter of the Russell Sage Foundation (which is an act of the state legislature of New York passed in 1907) described the foundation's purpose as "the improvement of social and living conditions in the United States of America," and it goes on to specify that it may use "any means to that end, which from time to time shall seem expedient to its members or trustees, including research, publication, education, the establishment and maintenance of charitable or benevolent activities, agencies and institutions, and the aid of any such activities, agencies, or institutions already established." The purposes of the Rockefeller Foundation, established in 1913, are even broader: "to promote the well-being of mankind throughout the world."

The bequest to the inhabitants of the town of Boston (and the parallel bequest to the corporation of the city of Philadelphia) made in Benjamin Franklin's will (1789) provides a striking contrast to this generalized beneficence and lack of detailed and legally binding mandates.[6] Franklin's codicil spells out the detailed requirement that the managers of his funds let out the principal "upon Interest at five percent per Annum to such young married artificers, under the Age of twenty-five years, as have served an Apprenticeship in the said Town and faithfully fulfilled the Duties required in their Indentures so as to obtain a good moral character from at least two respectable citizens who are willing to become their Sureties in a Bond with the Applicants for the Repayment of the Monies so lent with Interest according to the Terms hereinafter prescribed." Franklin went on to prescribe the exact form the bonds were to take, that the interest was to be paid annually together with a repayment of one tenth of the principal, upper and lower limits for the amounts of the loans to each applicant, what books and records the managers were to keep, and so forth. He went on to calculate that "if this Plan is executed and succeeds as projected without interruption for one hundred years," the principal would grow to £130,000. Of this, £100,000 was, at the end of the first century, to be paid out in public works, "such as fortifications, bridges, aqueducts, public buildings, baths, pavements, or whatever may make living in the town more agreeable." The other £30,000 was to be lent out, in the same way as before, to young artisans for a further hundred years. It was only at the end of this second century—by which time the principal would have grown to £2,061,000—that he left "one Million and sixty-one thousand pounds to the Disposition of the Inhabitants of the Town of Boston and Three Million to the disposition of the Government of the State not presuming to carry my views further."

Foundations, of course, continued to be established for specific purposes after the turn of the century. Indeed, many of Carnegie's smaller endowments were of the older, specific character; and as late as 1937, a large (if untypical) foundation, the Longwood Foundation, was established primarily to maintain the horticultural gardens of that name. However, in general, the American millionaires and their advisors were clearly worried that if they specified too exactly the purposes for which their foundations were established, these purposes would become anachronistic with the passage of time. In this they were obviously right. Social ills change with time. For example, tuberculosis was a major social ill at the beginning of this century, and controlling it loomed large among the objectives of the Russell Sage Foundation in its early years. Today, since the discovery of antibiotics, the disease does not have the same social importance.

Even before World War I, the feeling of confidence in the permanence of social and governmental structures that seems to permeate Benjamin Franklin's bequests to Boston and Philadelphia must have been badly shaken. By the end of the nineteenth century, the millionaires knew that they were living in a rapidly changing world. After all, they had themselves done quite a lot to change it.

Both of these developments—the desire to get beyond the symptoms to the root causes of social ills, and the broadening of the purposes of foundations so that they would have sufficient flexibility to change from one philanthropic purpose to another as circumstances demanded—were guiding principles in the establishment of the Russell Sage Foundation. Mr. de Forest, one of Mrs. Sage's advisors, in a memorandum discussing the proposed establishment of the foundation in memory of her husband, questioned "whether any foundation directed specifically to some single form of social betterment is wise as a permanent memorial intended to do good from generation to generation," and went on to say that "with the change and shift of social conditions, and extension, or maybe contraction, of the sphere of government activity, the future may develop other and greater needs for philanthropic action than any which are now apparent." He concluded that the foundation "should be sufficiently elastic in form and method to work in different ways at different times."

Other advisors spoke of the need for inquiry into the causes of ignorance, poverty, vice, and crime, and for devising methods of dealing with these problems. One of them, Mr. Brackett, suggested the need "for paying amply persons of marked experience and ability for making studies (with time for real study here and abroad) in the field of curative and preventive philanthropy with the aim of adding to that body of knowledge which shall help to lessen human wants and ills." The foundation historians conclude: "This consensus on the need for research and education must have accorded well with Mr. de Forest's own ideas. He shared the fresh enthusiasm of these early years of the twentieth century for hunting down the causes of poverty, disease, and crime, and discovering what could be done to eliminate or at least control those causes; the confidence that the large part of the human wants and ills in America was preventable and therefore would be prevented if only the facts about conditions and remedies were generally known."[7]

Margaret Olivia Sage was not unique among the founders of this period in her dependence on advisors for guidance in shaping the form and objectives of the foundation. John D. Rockefeller, Sr., relied heavily on the advice of Frederick Gates; and even Andrew Carnegie, who had very clear ideas of his own about philanthropy and how it should be administered, relied, according to Waldemar Nielson, on the advice of his friend and lawyer Elihu Root in establishing the Carnegie Corporation.[8] When Louis Bamberger and his sister Mrs. Felix Fuld were considering a multimillion-dollar endowment, they 'turned to Abraham Flexner for advice as to how the money could most profitably be used for philanthropic purposes. Flexner had already established himself as an authority with the Flexner Report, which had been commissioned by the Carnegie Foundation for the Advancement of Teaching and had provided the basis for a major Rockefeller Foundation program for medical education.

The distinctive characteristics of the foundations at the turn of the century appear to have been the result of interaction between the millionaires and this class of professional philanthropic advisors. Unlike the millionaires, many of whom came from impoverished families, the advisors came from well-to-do families, had good educations, often in law or religion, and were well-acquainted with social and educational developments in Europe, where many of them had traveled widely. Impressionistically, we can describe them as members of the East Coast establishment.

The millionaire founders were admittedly conscious of the responsibilities of wealth and the social problems their wealth might create. With a curious combination of brashness and public spirit, Carnegie spoke of the millionaire as a "trustee for the poor, intrusted for a season with a great part of the increased wealth of the community, but administering it for the community far better than it could or would have done for itself."[9]

As businessmen, they had learned to generalize their objectives. Carnegie had made his money originally from steel, and Rockefeller from oil, but both of them had branched out into general, large-scale corporate management, an area in which the objectives can be summarized into the single concept of profits and are not closely tied to a specific product. They sought a similar thrust for their philanthropic work, and it is likely that it was the advisors they turned to who found the solution to their problems by developing the concept of the general purpose foundation.

At the same time, one is rather struck by the absence of any burning zeal for particular reforms or a sharply focused sense of exactly what it is the public good demands. The millionaires wanted their money to do good, but that is about as far as they were prepared to mandate their trustees. One looks in vain for any equivalent to Dorothea Dix's passionate concern for the way the insane were treated in American asylums in the middle of the nineteenth century, or even Benjamin Franklin's more conservative but still clearly stated view that "good apprentices are most likely to make good citizens" and hence should enjoy the use (and the privilege of adding to the principal) of his bequests to Boston and Philadelphia. Robert H. Brenner, in writing of Carnegie's "gospel of wealth," suggests that "philanthropy was less the handmaid of social reform than a substitute for it. Wise administration of wealth was an antidote for radical proposals for redistributing property, and a method of reconciling the poor and the rich."[10]

The commercial corporation was to be the model for this "wise administration of wealth." Rockefeller spoke of "laying aside retail giving almost wholly and entering into the field of wholesale philanthropy." He drew the analogy with commerce even more closely when he asked, "If a combination to do business is effective in saving waste and getting better results, why is not combination far more important in philanthropic work?"

However mixed the motives of the millionaire founders may have been, these individuals, together with their advisors, managed to invent a new social institution—not a totally new form of institution, but a major variant of the old one—the distinctively American general-purpose foundation. The concepts and forms of organization that had been applied to private profit and had been the source of the wealth with which these foundations were endowed were in the general-purpose foundation applied to the public good, to philanthropic purposes generally. Therein lay the originality of the foundation. In earlier foundations, a specific purpose had been central to the institution. In fact, English common law (in contrast to American common law) required a specific and certain object, modified only by the doctrine of *cy pres* applied by the courts, for a trust to qualify for status as a charitable institution.[11] The older founders have often been as proud of the body of men (and surprisingly often women) they had managed to recruit for their purpose—whether this was the education of the young, the care of the sick, the pursuit of knowledge, or the preaching of the gospel—as they were of the actual cash endowments. These older foundations were essentially a body of people committed to some particular charitable service, and their financial resources were a necessary incidental that enabled them to live and pursue their vocation. The modern general-purpose foundations, however, are essentially a body of money committed to general charitable purposes, and their people (trustees and staff) are little more than a necessary incidental to insure that the money is properly managed and put to a good purpose. In general, corporate management in the service of good works was a distinctive contribution of the new institution; the parallels between these institutions and commercial corporations are clear enough.

But there is one very major difference between commercial and philanthropic corporations. The commercial body can use the tremendous unifying power of the concept of profits; the philanthropic body cannot. As long as philanthropic foundations had specific objectives, this difference was of no great importance. If the objective of a foundation was to provide baked potatoes at each meal to the students of Bryn Mawr, then there would be no great difficulty in evaluating how far that objective had been met. Similarly, if the foundation were established to loan money to young craftsmen in the expectation that it would be returned with interest, then it would not be too difficult to know whether one were carrying out the founder's intentions as efficiently as possible and how well his original expectations could be met. But how on earth is one to decide whether, of all possible courses of action, those on which a foundation has embarked are those best suited to carrying out a stated purpose to "promote the well-being of mankind throughout the world."

The Heyday of the Foundations

This question did not really bother either the founders or their advisors at the turn of the century. Kiger tells us that before World War I, "if any board were unanimous in regarding as socially desirable the spread of a given opinion, there was no hesitation in taking action in supporting its spread." However, after that war, and after the difficulties created by popular confusion about the relationship between Rockefeller's commercial and his philanthropic activities, foundations became more wary of taking up a position that might seem controversial or partisan. Kiger quotes Keppel (the head of the Carnegie Corporation at the time) as saying, "Surely the discovery and distribution of facts from which men and women may draw their own conclusions offers a field sufficiently wide and sufficiently vital to the welfare of humanity."[12] Nielsen tells us that for foundations, "the 1920s and 1930s were a time for thinking small and safe." What has happened is that caution, born of the political turmoil that greeted the establishment of the Rockefeller Foundation, has come to reinforce the simple belief of the founders of the early years of the century that, if only the root causes of social ills could be discovered, then poverty, disease, and ignorance could be rooted out. Not only was research the best strategy for doing good, it was also the one calculated to generate the fewest waves.

It is worth pausing to contemplate the incredible notion that mankind could actually discover the root causes of social phenomena. Such an assertion of the power of the human intellect was unprecedented, although the audacious claims of the founders of the American Republic that self-government could come from human hands, that mankind could, by itself, create the institutions under which it would live (and know enough about the defects of such institutions to anticipate and control them) were themselves unprecedented. These individuals imagined that, not mere epiphenomena, not surface postures, not the encrusted layers of tradition, but the real thing, the Archimedean level of social life, the root and branch causes could be reached and controlled. Such ideas were instrumental in the genesis of the great foundations around the turn of the century. In a wearier and warier time, one may look back with wry amusement to the discussion at the first meeting of the trustees of the Carnegie Endowment for International Peace on what they would do with all that money when peace broke out. This outrageous optimism was not entirely misplaced. The overall result of this casual confidence was to set some foundations off on a dual course of sponsoring research and (occasionally) acting on the results.

Indeed, why do we smile at this sort of earnest effort? Because it might be too costly in terms of money or political support. Because one might not be certain when the true cause was found, if one ever were, that controls would be efficacious, or even if they could be, that government or society would be willing to change. But we are running ahead of our story, reading back the lessons of a more skeptical time. Let us hearken to the beat of a different drummer, when there were still worlds to conquer and a little money and knowledge went a long way.

What we see emerging from these different, and to some extent contradictory, trends are the knowledge-oriented (hereafter, more simply, knowledgeable) foundations like Rockefeller, Carnegie, and Russell Sage. Their era of opportunity ran from the turn of the century through the beginning of World War II, roughly 1900 to 1940, from one optimistic Roosevelt to another. Within this period the focus on knowledge becomes progressively sharper. The idea of action based on knowledge of the root causes of social ills is an integral part of their approach from the beginning, but in the early stages research and direct action on the problems research has revealed ran hand in hand. Gradually, however, government comes to dominate the action and particularly the smaller foundations, like Russell Sage, come to rely not on their own resources but on those of government for direct action and increasingly devote their efforts to the production of knowledge on which government can act. We are concerned with relating the state of research, the size of resources, and the scope of interest among the three constituencies that would necessarily matter most to an aspiring, knowledgeable foundation—government, universities, and other foundations.

Throughout most of the first 40 years of this century, until the last few years at least, government could be described as limited in scope, poor in resources, and lacking in knowledge. It was confined largely to traditional functions, such as defense, justice, parks, and promotion of business. It spent what would now be considered a tiny proportion of the Gross National Product. Its lack of anything except narrow technical expertise was made more tolerable by its extremely limited aspirations. Universities were admitting only small numbers of students. They were poor in research facilities and lacked ambition for social change. Research institutes were scarce, and think tanks devoted to public policy were nonexistent. There was no "knowledge industry," as it is called today, with its symbiotic relationship to government, and its crisscrossing and overlapping centers, projects, and studies. Government did not do much, and knowledge did not have much to do with it.

Into this virgin territory—simple, naive, and unspoiled, by today's standards—came the knowledgeable foundation. Compared with what it was later to become, it was small in size and sophistication; but in relation to government and universities, it was comparatively large in the help it could offer. How sweet it was! In this time of institutional underdevelopment, America was, for the knowledgeable foundation, truly the land of opportunity.

Into spaces only lightly filled by government Carnegie went with its libraries, and Russell Sage with its sponsorship of physical culture in what was called the "playground movement." Luther Gulick, among others, served Russell Sage as an institution builder, loaning out its people for a few years to help start Campfire Girls and other worthy organizations. As a rule, beneficiaries were grateful for being helped, not furious at being taken over. When Russell Sage sponsored the first Regional Plan for the New York area, and the Regional Plan Association along with it, these activities were not considered futile efforts to create a nonexistent clientele for dubious master plans but rather part of the welcome wave of the future.[13]

To spend there must be spenders; hence the drive toward institutional development. To spend knowledgeably, there must be knowledge producers; hence the emphasis on elaborating the infrastructure of research universities and institutes. The Flexner report helped restructure medical education, and John D. Rockefeller's University of Chicago and Rockefeller Institute promoted high-level education and research. Mary Richmond at Russell Sage reoriented social work education and practice. By improving education, knowledgeable foundations were also promoting the knowledgeable people who would work with them.

There were other factors, too, that contributed to the self-confidence of knowledgeable foundations in the first half of the century. The idea that there were definable and separable roles for the spheres of government and private philanthropy was widely accepted, at least as a desirable aim. Nobody could really question the need for private philanthropy. As we have already noted, the trustees and staffs of the foundations—in some cases the very advisors who had helped develop the institutions in the first place, and in others their successors—appear to have come, for the most part, from a cohesive East Coast establishment. It is characteristic of an "establishment" that the credentials of its members are rarely questioned and that they share, along with other influential individuals in society, a considerable measure of agreement as to where the public interest lies. To a great extent, the route that progress would take in the United States could be gauged by looking across the Atlantic. Flexner in particular seems to have been heavily influenced by European examples: He used German models for his report on medical education and All Souls College in Oxford as a model for the Institute for Advanced Study in Princeton, of which he was the first director.

Despite the altogether too brief nature of this historical survey, the reasons for characterizing the first part of the twentieth century as the heyday of the American knowledgeable foundation are now evident. At a time of institutional and theoretical under-development, the potential "value added" (as economists would say) of strategic small sums was enormous. The chances of making a fundamental discovery, of creating a new institution or remodel-ing an older one, of making new beginnings, are necessarily greater before rather than after there are many competitors—or even vested interests—on the scene. Just as Ferdinand DeMara, "The Great Impostor," could practice almost any profession in remote places where it was unlikely that other professionals would be around to question his credentials, so did knowledgeable foun-dations benefit from being on the scene before they had formidable rivals.

The Seeds of Disenchantment

If Andrew Carnegie really thought that philanthropy would be a substitute for social reform, then the performance of foundations in the first decades of the century must have been disillusioning. In order to acquire leverage, foundations frequently made it a condi-tion of their grants that they be matched by government support. Indeed, Andrew Carnegie himself frequently made his gifts of library buildings conditional on a commitment from the local community for the library's upkeep. The Rockefeller Sanitary Commission, in its work on the control of hookworm, committed itself to "working through governments." Nielsen tells us that "the General Education Board was even more unrestrained in its ap-proach to government." Its initial aim was to encourage a more adequate system of public schools throughout the South. But as a base of popular support was lacking, so the board decided to sup-port "in every state, attached to the state university, a trained specialist in secondary education—a man who could inform, col-laborate, and guide professional, public, and legislative opinion. These missionary professors lobbied for new legislation in the southern states and went on numerous speaking tours in support of school-bond issues.... This period [up to 1920] was the epic time of intervention for the major American foundations. The rapidity with which they discovered the full array of means for influencing government, and the lack of inhibition with which they pursued this course is, even in retrospect, difficult to comprehend."[14] If Ben Whitaker is to be believed, "Russell Sage Foundation's investigations of money lending resulted in New York passing laws which prohibited several of the practices by which Mr. Sage had amassed his fortune."[15]

The very trends toward which the knowledgeable foundations were contributing—an increasing understanding of social problems as manageable rather than merely inevitable and the assumption by government of activities initiated by foundations—were the very trends that began to undermine their rationale. In trying to get at the root causes, they were undermining their own foundations as it were, the monopoly on money for hiring expertise.

In their early days, foundations were in the enviable position of being too small to be troublesome and yet large enough to appear helpful. They contributed ideas and knowledgeable staff to government. But once government had its own cadre of specialists, it would also have its own ideas on public policy. Once the government assumed an activity previously undertaken by foundations, the field for foundations was narrowed. Nielsen tells us that during the New Deal, as the federal government rapidly came to be the center of social action, the foundations were squeezed out by "the sheer magnitude of government programs." It is not only in social action today that the government occupies the center of the stage, but also in education, in health programs, in scientific, medical, and social research, in other words, in almost all the traditional fields of philanthropy, save only (in the U.S.) religion, from which it is barred by a peculiarity of the American constitution.

At the turn of the century, total public expenditure on social welfare programs (federal, state, and local) amounted to approximately 2.5 percent of GNP, but of this, the overwhelming majority was spent on education (primarily state and local expenditures)[16] and on veterans' programs. Although we have no comprehensive figures for foundation grants at this period, it seems likely that, except for these two areas, foundations had the field almost to themselves. Even by fiscal 1928-29, federal expenditure on social welfare under public programs was still only $798 million, and all but $140 million was accounted for by veterans' programs.[17]

Leaving aside the veterans' programs, we may compare the resources allocated by government with the resources allocated by the foundations for social welfare. In 1929, foundation income from endowments amounted to over $82 million[18] or 59 percent of federal welfare expenditures, excluding veterans' programs. In 1930, the amount was $94 million, or 63 percent of federal welfare, excluding veterans' programs. Figures for earlier periods are not readily available, but it seems probable that the proportion was at least as high until the Great Depression hit the American economy in 1931. After the Depression, two things happened. First, foundation income slumped from $80-$90 million per annum to $60-$70 million per annum. But second, and much more important, federal expenditures (still excluding veterans' programs) more than quadrupled between 1933 and 1934 and increased by a factor of more than 12 between 1932 and 1934. As a result, foundation income, which we may assume had been running at over 50 percent of federal welfare expenditures, fell dramatically to 3 percent and remained around the 3-4 percent level until the end of World War II. No wonder the foundations felt "squeezed out by the sheer magnitude of government programs."

Indian Summer

After World War II, the foundations were to enjoy an Indian summer. The fall season of the knowledgeable foundation opened with a glorious prospect. There were more of them, and they were bigger and better than ever. The maturing of fortunes, coupled with the taxation of estates, led to the emergence of giant foundations, symbolized best by the brass and brick Ford Foundation building, evidently designed to last forever. No bank was more solid; moreover, no bank maintained its own internal evergreen garden, not a mere repository, but a self-perpetuating source of life with its own source of energy. The stock market was buoyant and so were the foundations, many of which abandoned the safe-but-stodgy financial practices of the past to enjoy the boom that seemingly would never end. Upward and onward.

The subjects supported by foundations evoked the perceived needs or, if you will, the fashionable views of the time. When

America appeared to be resting on a firm foundation, but other countries appeared to be shaky, then foreign area centers sprang up all over. When America appeared to be in trouble, emphasis shifted to problems of poverty and race. The happiest partnership was struck with the producers of knowledge who, if they did not exactly inherit the earth, found in foundations a promised land. For as foundations flourished, they supported the scholars and the universities which could keep them supplied with projects and programs and spending.

As fast as foundations grew, however, government grew faster. But in the expansionist mood of the times, this was no obstacle; rather, it was an opportunity. Foundations could no longer do all or most of what was necessary, but if they were knowledgeable, they could, in the fashionable phrase of the period, "prime the pump" so that rivers of tax dollars would flow. If this were to be considered an accomplishment, where would one find sufficient praise for the Albert and Mary Lasker Foundation (of advertising fame) that masterminded the National Institutes of Health, whose funds expanded from a few million at the end of World War II to over a billion in two decades?

The operational embodiment of the knowledgeable foundation was found in its major criterion for success: getting the government to take over, on a larger scale, an idea or activity it sponsored. Bigger was better, apparently, for foundations as well as for government. The false dawn of the knowledgeable foundation was passing.

The Winter of Discontent

The second worst thing that can happen to anyone is to not get what one wants. The worst thing that can happen is to get what one wants and then find that it is not good. There was a time in the 1950s when many thought the heavens would applaud the good works wrought by federal billions for education, medicine, transportation, and housing. The money came, but it did not conquer. Whenever government tried to change deeply rooted human behavior (health habits, reading abilities, criminal tendencies), it risked a high rate of failure; the movement for the evaluation of governmental agencies, led by the Russell Sage Foundation, showed that our ability to measure failure far outstripped our capacity to cause success. What government could (and did) do was to reallocate its resources. Whereas in 1960 some 20 percent of the federal budget was devoted to social welfare programs and around 45 percent to defense, today the proportions have essentially been reversed. Government could claim, at least, that it had done what so many had urged it to do: namely, to reorder its priorities. But foundations could not make the same claim.

To the degree that knowledgeable foundations were concerned with expanding governmental social programs (which was considerable), they shared the blame when these seemed to be failing. Those foundations that concentrated on the development and dissemination of knowledge (Russell Sage spent the bulk of its money supporting sociology and spreading social science to the legal and medical professions) escaped these condemnations. But those that engaged in direct action—such as the decentralization disputes of Ocean Hill-Brownsville, pitting black residents against white teachers—became increasingly unpopular in some circles. What was worse, these circles were in government with positions of their own to protect, as well as powers to wield against foundations.

Whether the complaint was that foundations did too much (becoming meddlesome social reformers without electoral sanction), or too little (by supporting or by actually being part of the establishment that stifled reform), the result was the same: governmental sanctions designed to enforce better behavior. One point of view was that since foundations were funded by money that otherwise would have been taxed, it was really public income and should have been subject to the same discipline. As we have seen, when taken to a logical extreme, this argument would make foundation activity identical with government activity, which is the only authoritative expression of public will. Another argument was that foundations should be made responsive to the public will by opening up their activities to public scrutiny and their boards to representative trustees. Since the only authoritative expression of public desires is through government, this argument leads in the same direction as the previous one: to make foundations responsive would be to make them, ipso facto, redundant.

The surface manifestations of foundation malaise should now be clear: superfluous if they act like government, and damned if they do not. If foundations adopt the position that they should do whatever government does not, they bite the hand that feeds them. If they adopt the position of doing the same as government, it becomes unnecessary for them to be fed. Besides, the observation that the poor will always be with us, that serious problems will remain even after all those billions have been spent (whether by foundation or government does not matter), lends an air of discouragement to foundation activity. Why bother? To paraphrase the great Karl Marx, if anyplace foundations go is the wrong place to be, why go anywhere?

Before we try to answer this question, it is worthwhile to try to understand why foundations have come to this pass. In the beginning, they were favored because they were absolutely small, but relatively large, compared with government. It was good to be both inconspicuous and influential. It is not so good now to be absolutely larger and relatively smaller. For now, foundations find that they are more visible and less powerful vis-à-vis government. And however thin foundations stretch themselves, they can never match the ever-expanding scope of government, so that their capacities relative to almost any area of government are still deceptive. Hence the law of diminishing foundation returns: The more foundations work in the same areas as government, the less influential and the more vulnerable they become.

But what about those increasingly hard-to-find pieces of turf to which government has not yet staked a claim? In any reasonable democratic political system, we would expect government to appropriate those policies that combine popularity with feasibility. Then what is left for our favorite foundation? Evidently, the unfeasible and unpopular. If foundations are feeling a bit stuck out on the fringes these days, it is perhaps because they have been feeding on slim pickings for some time.

The causes of foundation difficulties are neither strange nor sinister; they are rooted in their asymmetric development in relation to government. Whether one believes that foundations have been too successful or that they have not been successful enough, it is clear that, for the moment, life has passed them by. They cannot prosper either by being absorbed into government or by being anathema to it. If foundations are a moveable feast, the great question is: Where should we move them?

The Third Sector
Foundations form part of what the Filer Commission described as

the "third sector" of American society, in contrast to the public or government sector on the one hand and the private or commercial sector on the other. It is a small third. The Filer Commission figures would make all forms of private philanthropy account for something on the order of 2 percent of the GNP, and of this, 7.25 percent is accounted for by foundations. This may be a vast sum in absolute terms, but it is still less than 0.2 percent of the GNP. We can call it a third sector, because, unlike the public sector, it is free of the discipline of the ballot box, and unlike the commercial sector, it is free of the discipline of the marketplace. Its ultimate justification for existence is its ability to seek to remedy, or to compensate for, the defects of those two great systems of societal control.

The need to take corrective action in circumstances in which market mechanisms are defective—monopoly situations and the like—has long been appreciated. In their early days, foundations were much concerned with correcting such distortions, particularly in the labor markets. For example, before World War I, the Russell Sage Foundation was conducting investigations into the working conditions of women; it gradually broadened the scope of its Committee on Women's Work to form, in 1916, the Division of Industrial Studies, which dealt with fundamental industrial problems affecting both men and women. The same concern for groups which lacked the clout to operate effectively in the marketplace seems to have inspired Russell Sage to institute the Division of Remedial Loans, which was concerned with protecting (guarding against the activities of loan sharks) and promoting the interests of small borrowers. This division not only carried out investigations into usurious practices but actively gave financial backing to institutions such as the Chattel Loan Society of New York, which provided loans for purchases, such as household furniture, to borrowers who otherwise would not have had access to respectable institutions in the money market.

Apart from seeking to correct market defects, nonprofit foundations could undertake projects which were too long-range for the commercial sector. For example, when the Russell Sage Foundation decided to finance the development of Forest Hills Gardens, a community in Queens, New York, designed to serve as a model of town planning, it was not, at first sight, engaging in an activity appreciably different from those normally undertaken by commercial property developers. However, the fact that similar developments in England at roughly the same period (such as the Hampstead Garden Suburb) also required a non-profit-making organization to take the initiative, coupled with the fact that when the Russell Sage Foundation finally sold out 13 years later it did so at a loss, suggest that the payoff for this development was too long-range for the commercial sector at the time. Had the Russell Sage Foundation hung on to the Forest Hills Gardens development—perhaps as long as another 20 years—the development might have been commercially successful. It may well be that today, since commercial enterprises have greater resources, they are also capable of undertaking investments of this range. But it is still true that the nonprofit foundation's freedom from the need to show results (a return on the investment) relatively soon provides it with a way in which it can serve the public interest that is not open to the commercial sector. The "green revolution" so closely identified with the Rockefeller Foundation provides an example of a development that was initiated by foundations, then taken up by both the commercial and public sectors, and then returned to foundations for fresh impetus and new directions. Similar examples could be found in the field of medical research, particularly in research on contraception.

Other more serious defects of the economic system—inflation, unemployment, trade cycles—have also provided and will endlessly continue to provide scope for foundation research, if not for foundation action. And this is as it should be; foundations, after all, are created out of the surpluses produced by business enterprise. Whether remedying economic defects is regarded as conscience money, or as "selling the system" by mitigating its excesses, or even as an attempt to express gratitude for past favors in the form of good works, the close connection between private foundations and private enterprise is natural and inevitable. All three of these justifications are at least implicit, when they are not explicit, in Carnegie's "gospel of wealth."

Foundations, the Economy, and Government

When they first appeared on the American scene, foundations had one main objective: to act directly to meet public needs or ameliorate social ills. Whether, as with the earliest foundations, the objective was specific, or as with those at the turn of the century, the objective was flexible and generalized philanthropy, the rationale was the same. There were "public goods," the demand for which could not be satisfied by private enterprise. But private 'enterprise generated surplus wealth that could be used to satisfy those needs, so long as those entrusted with that surplus were wise enough to use it in that way, either by personal philanthropy or, more efficiently, by establishing philanthropic foundations. At this time, government was expected to provide only a limited range of "public goods"—such as defense and the maintenance of law and order. It is doubtful whether this concept could ever have been fully operational, as it must have been clear very early that even the wealthiest philanthropist of the best endowed foundation could do little more than attack the fringes of the problem.

However, combined with this limitation was, as we have said before, the optimistic belief that the root causes of social ills—poverty, ignorance, crime, and disease—could be discovered and prevented if only the facts were known. From this belief sprang what we have called the knowledgeable foundations. Unlike Carnegie and the adherents of his gospel of wealth, the knowledgeable foundations and the professional managers who were then in charge of their policies were not antagonistic to government action. They researched or commissioned research on matters that needed to be put right. Sometimes they would act themselves on their research findings, but quite often they would leave the action to others—usually government. Or they used the tail-that-wags-the-dog approach, taking small steps which they anticipated government would follow with big steps.

It is impossible to ascribe precise time periods to these two stages of foundation activity. Different foundations adopted different strategies. For example, Russell Sage from its very beginnings emphasized research, but it was not until after World War II that it virtually abandoned the attempt to act directly to remedy the social ills that its research uncovered. Nonetheless, in very broad terms, we can see the direct action strategy—i.e., doing what government would not—as dominant until World War I, and the strategy of acting as a catalyst for government activity as dominant after the New Deal. As government began to regulate industry, sometimes with foundation inspiration, it took over the task of domesticating (and also of legitimating) business.

In any case, the original comforting notion that foundations should do what neither government nor industry would do ceased to be an adequate rationale for foundation activity by the time of the New Deal, if not earlier. The rationale that took its place was pluralism. Paul Ylvisaker has suggested that "foundations in their role of donors represent a private version of the legislative process —a deliberative process that selects goals, sets values, and allocates resources. The donee part of philanthropy is the counterpart of the administrative process in government, an alternative vehicle for getting things done."[19]   Of course, he could have drawn an equally good analogy with commercial enterprise, which is also a deliberative process that selects goals, sets values, allocates resources and is also a method of getting things done not necesarily any less effectively than the administrative process in government. But why, having two methods of getting things done, should we need a third? The classic pluralistic answer given by Martin Landau is that society, like any other self-organizing system, needs redundancy: "If there is no duplication, if there is no overlap, if there is no ambiguity, an organization will neither be able to suppress error nor generate alternative routes of action."[20] The related concepts of pluralism and redundancy are so crucial to the rationale of foundations, so seductive and at the same time so slippery, that they require more searching scrutiny.

Varieties of Pluralism

At its simplest level, pluralism can reflect no more than the need for several approaches to a problem. Facts, their interpretation, and the strategies to be derived from them are all subject to uncertainty. The more strings we have to our bow, the better our chances that if one breaks we will have a spare. Let us call this "procedural pluralism." By supporting a wide variety of projects, foundations could hope that some would work, even though each one had a low probability of success. And since foundations were not independent centers of expertise and depended instead on outside advice, they could try some of this and some of that (a plurality of approaches) without claiming to know in advance which was best. Alas, this procedural pluralism ("Let a hundred flowers bloom," so to speak) requires redundancy not only in approaches but also in resources. Capital contraction has not been good for procedural pluralism. The failure of capital to appreciate in the last decade means that foundation portfolios have not even kept pace with inflation, which reduces the real resources at foundations' disposal. Instead of pointing to a plurality of approaches, foundations must bet on a single one. Instead of protecting themselves and their projects on the ground that a high error rate is appropriate to a pluralist procedure, foundation officials must show that their judgment is right the first time.

The financial constraints on procedural pluralism are bringing to the surface previously submerged questions about the qualifications of foundation staff. That they are neither at the front line of action in government nor at the source of ideas in the academies and analytic institutes has long been a source of frustration for foundation officials. The most interesting conversations, they acknowledge, take place elsewhere. The opportunity to act as a broker between the world of ideas and the world of action without having to make a commitment to a correct course of action, has, however, eased the pain. Nonetheless, there is an implicit contradiction between generality and power: If diversity is desired, then generalists should serve, presumably without prejudice or preparation. But if expertise is required to reduce error because there are fewer finances, then why not get experts? Carrying the argument a step further, why not specialize in a single area in order to gather inside the foundation special sources of expertise? The Foundation for Child Development, which has a self-explanatory specialty, and the Markle Foundation, which is concerned with the mass media, are both examples of this tendency. Russell Sage's use of distinguished scholars as program directors (which intensifies its traditional direction) represents a somewhat different approach to the problem of increasing expertise to reduce error. It also seeks to capitalize on an advantage the knowledgeable foundation may have over the agencies financed from public funds in the quality of the relationship between research workers and administrators they are able to establish. Because public officials must stick to publically defensible regulatory guidelines, it is difficult for public officials to establish a participatory or collegial relationship with the investigators whose research they are funding. These are only a few harbingers of the changes that may follow from the financial constraints under which foundations now have to operate.

Leaving aside financial constraints, why cannot foundations

take their stand with policy pluralism, the notion that it is, ipso facto, desirable to have different approaches to the same sort of policy? The difficulty is not only (as it first appears) that government does so much, but that it already does whatever it is doing in many different ways in many different places. The plain truth is that government is already rife with redundancy. After all, has it not been the theme of numerous commissions on governmental reorganization, from Taft's at the turn of the century to Carter's today, that there is an excess of overlap and duplication. The reasons for this redundancy need not detain us long: Government cannot be organized on every basis at once; different periods bring different justifications for organizational ambitions; for example, whether the health or education of Indians should be left to the Bureau of Indian Affairs rather than HEW depends on our problem focus. The simple fact is that doing something a little differently probably means doing what government already does elsewhere.

Following the motto "If you can't beat 'em, join 'em," foundations could adopt the same role as the expanding government—the bigger the better—big foundations and even bigger government. The critical function would be exercised by getting government to grow gracefully in this direction rather than that. It would not be difficult for foundations to become, in effect, an adjunct of government, filling in the interstices in programs, bringing people together who find official contact awkward, justifying what would, in any event, be done. Gradually, imperceptibly, foundations would filter into government, providing a quantum of flexibility, or an aura of respectability, or a place, perhaps, to begin or end a career in government. The prospect is hardly elevating. Nor are there encouraging precedents. On previous occasions when foundations appeared to get too close, in effect acting as advisors to a particular administration, they soon found they could not stand the heat and had to leave the political kitchen.

To go from one extreme to another, the policy pluralism approach might be replaced by the policy perversity approach: Do whatever government would not like. A conservative form of perverse pluralism might spawn a call for abandonment of the welfare state, and a radical form might ignite a demand for complete equality of income and wealth. An intermediate form would be to mount a frontal attack on the size of government: Government should get smaller, even if it cannot get smarter; proposed governmental programs should replace, rather than add on to, existing ones that should not be abolished entirely.

If the policy pluralism approach would leave one wondering why foundations needed to do something government is going to do anyway (and perhaps better), then the policy perversity approach would leave one wondering how foundations could expect to get away with biting the hand that, if it does not exactly give, can surely take away. Surely there must be a position between "it need not" and "it cannot" be done.

Indeed, there are several. We need only mention one: the growth of community foundations. These represent a major effort to escape the dilemma by focusing foundations on state and local levels of government which have far fewer resources and are also undersupplied with a wide range of information.

But a more systemic approach is needed for foundations that are national in scope. In this winter of their discontent, it is time for foundations to reexamine their basic premises. Thinking about foundations—for ideas are the proper place for the knowledgeable foundation to begin—has proceeded from the historically derived assumption that their role was to make up for those deficiencies of the market economy that government itself could not be induced to undertake. But the rise of big government has undercut the normally accepted rationale of foundations: Pluralism has a hollow ring when all it means is doing what government does a little differently.

Fortunately, there is a conception of pluralism that is not based on redundancy in means and approaches but instead on a plurality of values and a concept of balance, which has long been recognized as integral to the question of governmental power in society. Worried about the possibility of tyrannical majorities, the founders of the American constitution sought to disperse power among different electoral constituencies and branches of government, a scheme that goes under the names of "separation of powers" and "checks and balances." James Madison saw in a federal republic a means of increasing the diversity of interests so that no one interest could easily overpower the others.

And so it has proved to be, at least until recently. A federal structure under which there are at least two of everything, from legislatures to executives to judiciaries, seemed to spawn diversity. But now, as government becomes by far the nation's largest employer, as it directly takes around a third of the national product, and through its regulations directs substantial amounts of putatively private expenditures, questions about the balance of forces in society are bound to grow in importance. Perhaps it is time to look at the inherent weaknesses of government, as we still do for markets, to see whether and where knowledgeable foundations might still play a useful role.

Even if one were to agree with this argument, it would not necessarily follow that it is the special province of foundations to safeguard and promote a balance of powers. Why should this third sector take a special interest in the balance between the other two and citizens in society at large?

In one way, the question almost answers itself. The self-interest of philanthropic foundations, if nothing else, suggests that their autonomy depends on not being overwhelmed, either by government or by industry. When the main threat appeared to come from industry, including family founders, pluralistic balance might suggest building up government as a counterweight. (This may still be the situation in some places.) But now, as the private economy declines in power, we can expect future fears to focus on government. In foundations, nowhere is this more evident than in relation to the Internal Revenue audit, which appears to evoke the same emotions as hellfire and brimstone did in old sermons. The possibilities for punitive action by government against foundations have been vastly exaggerated. This scaredy-cat syndrome is a commentary more on excessive internal fear than on real external threat. Aside from its salutary provision for better public accounting and its requirement that foundations actually use a modest portion of their assets to do something useful (hardly an act of suppression), all the Act of 1969 does is to impose a rather too high excise tax (4 percent instead of the 2 percent required for auditing) which, though slightly onerous, is hardly confiscatory. The circumstances of the time do suggest that foundations will get into trouble if they engage directly in electioneering; but that hardly seems a loss because, first of all, they would probably not be very good at it and second, it would make them even more like government than they are now.

No, such danger as there is comes not from the threat of abolition but from the threat of absorption, not from overt hostility, but from the all-too-loving embrace. Whereas industry is concerned with avoiding attack and cares, if at all, only that good appears to be done, government is actually concerned with the substance of foundation activity.

Foundations are not the only ones, by far, whose interests are implicated in the balance between big government and big industry. Citizens may well wonder what their participation means in an era of institutional dominance. There are concerns about personal privacy and group opportunity. Whether from lack of governmental protection or from an excess of it, human rights are at issue, abroad as well as at home. The very survival of independent education and commercial culture, beset by a lack of resources and a growing dependence on government, is at stake. Might there not then be alternatives to corporate dominance and bureaucratic procedures for providing collective responses to social issues? And might not foundations, cut adrift from industry and not yet subservient to government, play a key role in fostering those alternatives?

Needed: A New Intellectual Rationale for Foundations

What we are suggesting is a change in relative emphasis. In the past (either from a desire to save capitalism or through an oedipal relationship to business), the main weight of foundation research was directed toward socioeconomic problems; it seems to us that the time has come to shift the emphasis more toward sociopolitical problems. We are not suggesting that foundations have ignored the problems created by political systems. There are many examples to the contrary, including the activities of Amnesty International or the Vera Institute, both of which have received funds from foundations. Rather, we are suggesting that the problems created by our political system have not received the same systematic analysis as the problems created by our economic system.

Analogies between the economic system of free enterprise and representative democracy have frequently been drawn. Schumpeter, for example, defined the democratic process as "that institutional arrangement for arriving at political decisions in which individuals acquire power to decide by means of a competitive struggle for the people's vote." Presumably, competitive political parties, by facilitating rotation of government officeholders, compensate for the failures of one government by providing another. It follows that foundations ought to have a special interest in political parties and in any other institution or process that either promotes competition among governments or that otherwise provides an arena for criticism of the government in office. Obviously, the media that convey this criticism, and the legal profession that is especially responsible for protecting proper procedures, deserve to take precedence.

But what of the deepest defects of the political system? To ignore government is only to pretend to live in another time. Economists have coined the technical term "market failure" to identify the circumstances in which market mechanisms are incapable of performing satisfactorily their usual function of allocating resources in accordance with public demands. Political scientists, though well aware of the weaknesses of government, have no exactly analogous concept. What such a concept needs to express is not merely the failure of a particular policy, activity, or product— were the fields of failure to include everything that does not work, it could be coextensive with human experience—but rather generic defects inherent in the system. For example, when smoke pollution in one area adversely affects people in another (with no adequate mechanism for compensation) this is a market failure (called an "externality"), because existing market mechanisms cannot fully capture the costs of pollution. When market failure occurs, the remedy always appears, explicitly or implicitly, to be government action. But if market failure is to be dealt with by government, then who is to deal with government failure?

This is not the time, nor would we have the space in this essay, to examine fully what government failure might mean. Instead, we must make do with illustrations. We might begin with the well-known "near-sighted time horizon." Government officials are most interested in the period until the next election. This sort of shortsightedness is, of course, complemented by the classic caution: "Do nothing for the first time" unless it is guaranteed to be popular. By refusing to stray from popular will, governments lose opportunities to try innovative policies that might prove to be even more popular.

Without claiming to counter government, it is possible for foundations to look into public mechanisms for error recognition and error correction. Government officials are generally skilled at choosing among alternative policies in terms of their first-order effects, but they usually ignore the second-order effects partly because they lie outside the "nearsighted time horizon." In considering a social policy—for example, some form of unemployment insurance—the first-order effects are amenable to existing forms of analysis, but the second-order effects—the effects on the structure of society—in general defy current forms of policy analysis.

In listing examples, we might go on to the "size solution"—government tries to solve its internal problems by allowing each internal element to expand—and we might end with the "clumsy giant" syndrome: When government takes over an activity, it tends to swamp the social support mechanisms that made the activity desirable in the first place. Parents see less need to support schools or neighbors to coalesce once government gets into the act.[21]

How might foundations cope with these alleged failures of government? Apparently, they should only fund proposals with long time horizons and a high risk of turning out badly, else government would probably take them on. Presumably then most foundation ventures should not succeed. Would this be, one wonders, counteraction to government failure, or a cover-up for foundation failure? How could foundations pit themselves against the size solution without diminishing their own powers, or cope with the clumsy giant without getting trampled? It is time to find out.

In concentrating on government failure, we should not forget to think of foundation failure. Evaluation, like charity, should begin at home. The success syndrome might be called a foundation failure. In order to gain credit for innovations without using up their entire budgets, foundations are likely to call for narrowly defined projects, whose costs are calculated on the marginal principle: just enough to do the job. The resources required by applicants for generating ideas, sustaining staff, and for their own development are left out of account. Without arguing the matter here, we can speculate that perhaps this "creaming" phenomenon may be a fundamental failure of foundations.

The original rationale for American foundations was that they would directly ameliorate social miseries or improve social functioning. Later, the rationale was modified, so that foundations conducted research into matters which someone else (i.e., the government) could directly ameliorate. Today, so many other people are also conducting this sort of research—indeed, government is spending huge amounts to finance those who will suggest new things for it to ameliorate—that it is time to move on to a third rationale. In their earliest days, foundations simply spent their money doing whatever they thought should be done. In their second phase, they adopted the tail-that-wags-the-dog approach. Today, it seems that they are themselves being wagged, and something new is needed.

That something, in our view, is a deliberate attempt to concentrate foundation resources on alternative ways of thinking about government. This means thinking not only about existing programs and activities but also about the inherent limits of government activity, just as we have learned to think about the inherent limits of economic activity. Foundations should, in short, make conscious use of their independence. They are not directed by the government concerning what they shall do (although they are regulated concerning how they shall do it). They need not be subjected to the committee/consultative method of making decisions about what should be done that characterizes universities (tails which are themselves increasingly wagged by the government, directly through its regulations and indirectly through the money which it can offer for doing the things it wants done). What foundations are uniquely free to do, if they will only rise to the occasion, is to think about alternative models for handling whatever it is that should be done without determining in advance who should do it, and to push their analysis to a deeper level than government or business has either the time or the incentive to do.

In short, foundations should become a site for alternative ways of thinking about problems, rather than the handmaidens of existing governmental or corporate attachments. In such a role, foundations would be building on the one relatively unique strength which they do (or at least could) have: their independence and their freedom from having to meet either political or market criteria. The price of such an approach would be a high degree of irrelevance to daily policymaking activity; foundations would produce large amounts of currently "irrelevant" knowledge. To us, this seems a price worth paying. At least it is worth arguing and disagreeing about.

3

Reaching for Answers

Landrum R. Bolling, George W. Bonham, McGeorge Bundy, James Douglas, Fred M. Hechinger, John H. Knowles, Waldemar Nielsen, B.J. Stiles, Aaron Wildavsky, Paul N. Ylvisaker

George Bonham: For anyone interested in the social contributions of foundations, the Douglas-Wildavsky position is certainly an excellent departure point, though by no means the only one. My suggestion is that we start from there, and then branch out into a broader inquiry of possible long-term roles for philanthropy in America.

John Knowles: I thought the Wildavsky-Douglas paper was well done within certain limits. But when they paint a picture of foundation malaise, I think they have missed the mark. I for one do not believe that charge is applicable to the large American foundations. I know it isn't true of the Rockefeller Foundation, and I think I can speak for my colleagues as well. To the contrary, the heat is always up in our kitchens. Like most other American institutions today, foundations are evaluating their roles, their efficiency, their results. Such work should obviously never stop, because we are constantly adapting to rapidly changing societal conditions, and periodic critical reassessment is necessary to any form of institutional health. I can assure you that we have our share of such reevaluation at the Rockefeller Foundation. Read our annual reports, if you don't believe it, and particularly the ones dated 1974 and 1978. Let me quote some paragraphs from my 1978 report:

> The board of trustees has conducted two extensive reviews over the past three years. The preliminary

results of a five-year program review initiated by the
president in late 1976 were also made available to them.

As a result of these extensive reviews, the board expressed serious concern about excessive diffusion of interests; the apparent lack of a unifying theme; an excessive burden on the trustees of reports and grant
descriptions, with too little time devoted to policy
discussions. The question was posed as to whether or
not the foundation should be continued or disbanded,
as were immediate questions concerning each of our
programs....

The recommendation that the RF should be continued
under present guidelines of overall expenditure was ap-
proved by the trustees with the feeling that the goose
that has laid so many golden eggs should not be killed.
Increased emphasis should be placed on seizing or re-
sponding to unusual opportunities through an increase
in flexible funds to pursue overarching issues involving
several or all of the foundation's program areas, such as
neglected aspects of: (1) the problems of unemployment
and inflation, and (2) the transformation of progress
and the transition from uncontrolled expansion to sus-
tainable growth in the developing countries.

I think the foundations have in fact done a good job of antic-
ipating the future and future societal problems and have used their
resources well in providing new avenues of approach for government and other institutions, including educational institutions. I
do not say this as some kind of introductory apologia or defensive
speech, nor am I overinflated with the idea that the foundations
are going to save the world. They are not. But I think that, overall,
the large foundations have a reasonable track record and have
proved their value in a country which, God help us, will continue
to value pluralism and heterodoxy.

I do think that all institutions in the United States are nervous. I
think the country is nervous, the leaders are nervous, and I think
that this general anxiety is particularly rife in foundations. There is
no other organization in the world where you are potentially going
to be burdened with more guilt or more uncertainty than in a foundation. Simply stated, this is because no other organization has the
freedom and flexibility to use money and expertise to improve the
human lot—there is no place to hide.

Imagine being a trustee of an organization that is charged with
spending $50 million a year to "improve the well-being of mankind

throughout the world"—the charter of the Rockefeller Foundation. Imagine being in a foundation today when massive sums of governmental money are being spent by de facto governmental foundations that never existed when we were first founded in 1913. Carnegie built libraries in this country. The Rockefeller Foundation went to work on hookworm down South. There was no HEW then. Now we have other problems.

Everyone seems to bring their pack of troubles to the foundations. They're all beset by inflation, and they all thought that the supply of money from Washington was guaranteed to increase endlessly. It may be Vernon Jordan of the Urban League, or Dick Lyman of Stanford. They have their problems. So do we and, obviously, in times of inflation, a foundation should, like any other institution, utilize sexless cost-benefit ratios and so-called zero-based budgeting and be willing to take its licking in inflation and assume its responsibility in trying to control it. Alas, we live in an age of numeracy, not literacy, and we have grown a bit cynical—knowing the cost but not the value of everything we do. Value judgments are as important as economic analyses.

The one regret I have had in the Rockefeller Foundation is that I didn't keep a tape going constantly from the first day I got here, so that a permanent record of the kinds of people that come here and the ideas they have would be available. I would also like to record the arrogant insults I have to listen to. I used to run a hospital. There, everybody knew they could run it better than I could, and they had personal experiences with it and that was very helpful. Half the time they were right and I was anxious to move on what they perceived as bad food, inadequate nursing, unnecessary surgery, overutilization of high-cost inpatient facilities, and so on. The other half was human foolishness and petulance and my job was to distinguish between the halves.

Here, everybody's an expert but most give you no more logical suggestions than you generate yourself by working 18 hours a day with a staff that spends full time just as worried about our responsibility as anybody who sits on our board or looks at us from the outside. So I do not see the foundations in a state of malaise. I think they have very substantial opportunities and, if they can recruit the best people, they'll add their bit to improve the lot of mankind.

A new social need is the issue of monitoring governmental programs and providing alternative ways of solving problems. I think that this element is a very positive aspect of the paper. This year, for example, we've had extensive discussions with Secretary of Labor Ray Marshall, a former Rockefeller Foundation fellow, by the way, and Juanita Kreps, Secretary of Commerce. The Department of Labor spends about $5 billion a year on unemployment in the United States, but they simply are unable to monitor or follow up what's happening to this wide variety of approaches. We're seriously considering, at their request, either adding a unit to an existing free-standing organization or actually establishing a new organization which will have that follow-up evaluation as its primary charge.

Fred Hechinger: I completely agree. I also think it's an excellent paper. My only divergence from its basic thesis, one of its central points, is the apparent apprehension that because government is doing infinitely more, there is therefore a real crisis in that there's nothing for the foundations left to do. I think that's just not so.

One of the problems I would not personally worry about is that anybody's doing too much, including the government, and that it therefore becomes more difficult for foundations to find a *raison d'être* for their own activities. The opposite is the case. Government *is* addressing itself to a lot of the big issues that in the past were dealt with primarily by the foundations, and therefore were dealt with rather ineffectively because the issues were essentially too big for even the big foundations.

It seems to me there is not less but more opportunity for the foundations to do an awful lot of things that we all know the government has neither the power nor the intention to do anything about. Or it does not have the political agreement—the political consensus. Government, after all, only acts on issues on which it can get political consensus. It stands to reason that an awful lot of areas in which such consensus doesn't exist remain for somebody else to deal with.

Now if foundations will be dealing with areas in which there hasn't been this kind of political consensus, this means almost automatically dealing with issues that are more controversial. Frankly, I don't weep over that prospect. If there is one organization in the United States that ought to be able to afford to deal with controversial issues, it is after all the foundation, which doesn't have to do the kind of accounting that virtually every other institution in America is now bound by.

George Bonham: If you talk about a redefinition of foundation functions, there are in my opinion social needs that are very difficult if not impossible to resolve except through government action. Lyndon Johnson was intent on beginning to resolve the problems of the inner city. I remember his appeal to corporations, particularly to insurance companies, to make an effort to rebuild the inner cities. Certainly, foundations have been very active in this area, though on the periphery. But in terms of very central philosophic and political issues, I haven't seen very much success, because of the enormity of the problem. Now are you saying that some of these massive social needs ought still to be the focus of foundation attention, since they're so difficult to resolve?

Fred Hechinger: I think the specific approaches or techniques for dealing with such problems ought to be very much the concern of the foundations. Obviously no foundation is going to save the inner cities. Eventually, if the inner cities can be saved or revitalized, the effort will have to come from a combination of government and the private economy. Or, depending on your political point of view, private economy aided by the government. The private economy deals with these problems in a very narrow sense and only in terms of what it can do while at the same time improving its own profitability, which is, I suppose, the way it ought to be.

The government has to do more than that. It has to pick its targets. And it has to find techniques that work. Now I don't think the government has ever been equipped to do that effectively, and it's for that purpose that the foundations are still very much needed.

Waldemar Nielsen: For the moment at least I'm more interested in what seemed to me the approach that Douglas and Wildavsky were taking. They try to reopen some questions about fruitful roles for foundations in the greatly changed context in which foundations operate today as compared with 30 and 40 years ago. I think that this is precisely the kind of question that all those, either in philanthropy or interested in philanthropy, or, for that matter, in universities and interested in universities, ought continuously to be asking.

Douglas and Wildavsky have put their finger on what is obviously the central change that has occurred in our national life in our adult lifetime—that is, the tremendous increase in the role of government in a whole range of areas in which private philanthropy, the private element in American life, has historically and traditionally concentrated its work. That is a massive and profound new fact in our national existence. Douglas and Wildavsky have raised a central question: namely, does this emergence—they call it the "era of big government," and I "the era of the welfare state"—change the foundation role? Government has moved into or has been pressed by public demand and public need into major activities in whole new areas in which either it once did not operate or operated only in a limited way, such as basic scientific research before World War II.

It seems to me that there are at least two other issues that underscore not only the relevance but really the centrality of the questions that are posed in this paper. One is that government has mucked up a great many of these major new enterprises that it has undertaken—not because of stupidity but because of overambition and overreaching, given the state of the art in many of these social areas. Government wildly misestimated the impact on medical costs, for example, of some of its well-intentioned efforts in the medical field. In the fields of housing and urban renewal also, government programs have produced many failures and sometimes appalling side effects. Nothing is more important than to try to get both a detached and a competent assessment of what went wrong in those situations. And to try to derive out of that some constructive suggestions of how, the second time around, things can perhaps be done somewhat better.

Many of the most agonizing problems in our national life, whether the safety of nuclear reactors or how to deal with a major urban redevelopment problem, are not the kinds of problems that a newspaper reporter can say anything very sensible about out of general knowledge. They are problems of such complexity and magnitude that they demand a combination of high talents, great technical capability, and, sometimes, considerable amounts of data and computerized research methods.

If you accept the premise that it's important for somebody other than government to take a look at these enormous undertakings, and what may have gone wrong, then it means that it has to be an institution with a certain scale of sophistication, and a certain scale of resources, to assemble the talents and to do the research that's necessary to say anything sensible or usable. The universities are certainly one major source of the kind of evaluation that I'm talking about. But foundations—and again I emphasize the big foundations—are almost peculiarly able to assemble those resources, to take a detached position, and to make a vital contribution to the national welfare by recognizing that one of their very important new roles in this era is to address themselves to the constructive criticism and evaluation of public policy.

There are two questions that I would like to add: First, how many foundations are really competent to undertake the kind of examination and analysis that I'm talking about? Even among the biggest ones I think there is some legitimate question that can be raised on the issue of competence. By competence I mean scale of resources as well as sophistication, qualifications of staff, and so on. We're talking here about a tiny percentage of the total number of foundations. It is simply not relevant to think that 28,000 of the 30,000 foundations in this country can do more than the very useful but very different kind of local and specialized things that they do.

The second question, the political one, is that if the big, competent foundations really seriously undertook in a major way to support such critiques and appraisals of public policy, could they get away with it? That is, how quickly would they get themselves blown out of the water politically because they would be treading on some very tender corns in every one of these issues? That is a large question. They are obviously not democratically elected and publicly accountable institutions in the conventional sense. If they presume, in effect, to attack some health insurance bill, let us say, by funding a critique of certain of its aspects, it would probably offend powerful political and public figures in American society. The foundations could encounter a storm of backlash as a result. The prescription that Douglas and Wildavsky have put forward, insofar as it is a valid prescription, applies probably only to a very few foundations, and even then only within defined limits.

George Bonham: John Knowles earlier referred to the certain nervousness that has recently existed among many foundations, and the understandable causes of it. I wonder myself how that nervousness, quite aside from its genesis, impinges on two of the important criteria of Douglas-Wildavsky for private philanthropy: long-time horizons and high-risk effort. My own impression is that those criteria actually are infrequently used. I don't find too many examples in fact. Even major initiatives that have contained only some element of risk are the exceptions.

On the contrary. I've found some major foundations that half the time don't really know what their program areas are. They always seem immersed in some cabal-like internal reassessment. Also, I am not very confident about their intellectual capability to take long-term positions.

Lastly, I would say that, speaking about accountability, very few foundations make any effort to assess their own risk taking, their own successes and failures. One of the few exceptions that I remember is a Ford Foundation report which was called "A Foundation Goes to School." This was really a remarkable effort in the political sense. But I see on the whole very little of that. So even when one spends moneys, the failures are well hidden. This is typical also of academic performance. We rarely know about the failures, only of successes. These may be somewhat minor criticisms of my own, but they relate these two criteria of long-time horizons and high risk.

McGeorge Bundy: I had a feeling about this paper that I often have when I read something that is clearly deeply felt and strongly argued. I thought the authors made an excellent case *for* what they wanted to do, and a lousy case *against* the things that they didn't want to do. I found on almost every page assertions about what foundations do and don't do that were simply false, at least in respect to the one that I know best. I also found what seemed to me a very dated view of the dangers the foundations face with respect to the political process. The experiences of 1968 and 1969, and our experience since then, seem to me to have taught a considerable number of the more sophisticated foundations how to do the things that they are doing. I would be very skeptical of any notion that foundations are in real political danger in the sense that Wally Nielsen just suggested, assuming that they behave with reasonable care in the way they go about whatever objectives they choose.

Actually, one of the interesting outcomes of the last decade is the development of 501 (c)3 organizations with very pronounced political biases which, as far as I can tell, remain unthreatened by political processes. So I would like to ask Douglas and Wildavsky whether they really intended to be quite as critical as they are of the intermediate processes like those which Ford and Rockefeller have now been engaged in for 20 years (and in Rockefeller's case for 40 years) in the field of agricultural research. In the end this effort has had a great effect on the way governments behave and has led to forms of government behavior that simply would not have occurred without the foundation initiative.

Those particular endeavors did have a long time horizon and did involve research, but they did not involve the kind of research that is briefly, imaginatively, and tantalizingly sketched in the last page of this paper. My own view would be that what the authors want to do is admirably worth doing, and that foundations should try to help, but that their proposal by no means exhausts the field of useful relationships between foundations and government.

Paul Ylvisaker: I read the paper twice, deliberately at different times, and come here neither to praise it nor to bury it. I think it is a very provocative paper. It forced me on the second reading to get beyond the quibbles and ask myself as well as the authors whether we could go all the way in the line of their argument, with their calling into question the sometimes presumption of reformist philanthropies that they could say what was good for society. I would agree experience has taught us to be more modest. But Douglas and Wildavsky then fall into the identical trap on the opposite side—by asking foundations to decide when government is doing badly by society. They now want to identify failures and avoid doing harm, which is exactly the same pretentiousness in reverse. But I count in their favor that they urge philanthropy to play an assertive role in the public process; "mixing it" in a pluralistic society has always been a healthy antidote to self-righteousness.

I would also argue that we ought to be much more tolerant of means in a very diverse and complicated society. To limit your repertoire of action or thought to one line of approach is wrong. Having arduously accumulated a variety of different devices for working with government, working against it, working with business, working against it, doing developmental things, doing research, or whatever, I would keep that whole bag of tricks rather than narrowing down to one, as I hear the authors advocate.

Foundations, as an advantaged leadership group within society's third sector, have responsibility for setting the pace, standards, and agenda for that sector. If they are to do that as they should, they have to acquire, they will acquire, and are acquiring a stature that is more independent and distinguishable from both business and government. Wealth associated with business still is obviously the most conspicuous source of funding. But I regard the departure of Henry Ford from the Ford Foundation board as symbolic—a statement that foundations have come of age. No longer does the business agenda dictate the parameters of philanthropy. (Interestingly, within 24 hours of his departure, I got calls from Japanese philanthropists, now so closely linked to corporate structures, asking what Ford's resignation might portend.)

With respect to government, Wildavsky and Douglas are saying that it has grown so monstrous that philanthropy should become its critic rather than junior partner. The halcyon days when philanthropy could dominate through better ideas and relatively sizable outlays are over. Now government is threatening the intellectual establishment by substituting regulation for financial aid. Witness the plaintive cries of foundations and universities—now so reminiscent of business years ago: The government is now becoming "our enemy" and this regulation that we used to propose for business is now being put on us and we don't like it. Both in our everyday outlook and in our modes of innovation, we are turning away from easier assumptions about governmental alliances and an identity of interests.

Therefore, we are moving toward philanthropy, logically and historically, as an independent force. The first implications are financial. How do you channel money into an independent sector that doesn't have its own revenue sources? It's either going to come from government or from business or rich people. The Filer Commission labored with that dilemma and came out with very puzzled answers. I frankly don't know what the solution is, except possibly to say, Play down the role of money in philanthropy. Money has been so conspicuously the name of the game. But there are other avenues to social influence; shifting and elevating behavioral patterns within philanthropy are clearly alternatives to raising more money.

Wildavsky and Douglas adopt that approach and argue for philanthropy to concentrate on a prophetic role. How often and how deeply can philanthropy bite the hand of government—when that hand has gotten so much stronger and tightened its regulatory leash? More than I would have thought a decade ago. That there are so many others suffering the same frustrations gives philanthropy more popular support and room for risk taking than one might expect.

Still, this is the major point that I'd like to drive home. I am puzzled by it and I'm not even sure my populist instincts provide the answer. I look ahead at the next 30 years; they are going to be extraordinary years. We'll be moving into the seven-billion-people world. An early intimation of this new world is the illegal immigration into the United States, now nearly a million a year. Our cities are quietly being repopulated by all manner of diverse cultures (though the Census Bureau doesn't count them). And as I look ahead, I keep hoping (like a French aristocrat, I suppose) for some De Tocqueville to give an optimistic analysis of what's on the other side of this gathering turbulence. I wonder whether philanthropy—and I include universities and education in this as well as the foundations—whether we're ready to frame or engage in the dialogue that has to be staged. How do you preserve the historic sense of decency and guarantees of human rights that we've accumulated over the past as we move quickly from affluence to scarcity, from some homogeneity, at least enough to enable us to write our Constitution and conduct our politics, to the new heterogeneity?

Is philanthropy ready for that kind of dialogue? Will it speak independently? The Douglas and Wildavsky paper, I think, is a little provincial on this count: It doesn't talk about the international context. It talks only as though we were going to continue within a closed system and an underlying political consensus. Also, I think our selection for this exercise is very revealing. Look at the homogeneity around this table. I needn't belabor the all too obvious: no blacks, no women, no Hispanics, no one from the developing world. But more than that, within each of us there must be a sense of what has to be taken into account in that dialogue—some representation of the widening divergence in economic status and human values that are emerging as cultural facts of life, both on the international and domestic scenes.

The most significant thing that I think is coming out of Harvard these days is not the dialogue over back to basics in the curriculum but the entry of Hispanic students, like blacks 10 years ago—incipient leaders who will be the Vernon Jordans of that burgeoning cohort of American society, wondering as they move from barrio to prominence: Should they live within the system as they find it, or follow more angry logics of the rising disadvantaged? The choice may be predictable for such as come to Harvard—and to the foundations. But the question is framing the dialogue of our times, and philanthropy may be too removed from emerging realities to handle or much influence it.

We may have the right values, but not the right perceptions, posture, or credibility. I don't know whether or how quickly we can adapt. It won't happen simply by having more Hispanics and third-worlders on our governing boards. Wildavsky and Douglas would have us grope in another direction—that of setting different agendas and thinking in other dimensions.

I remember happily an occasion when such a departure was made. When Terry Sanford got stuck in the second half of his term as the one-term governor of North Carolina, he came to the Ford Foundation and said, in effect, I've got the consent of at least enough people in my state so that the Ford Foundation can come down and help devise a transitional process for getting us out of an evolutionary dead end. We have not been dealing with a relevant social agenda; existing processes don't allow blacks to participate, and without their participation we have neither full wisdom nor credibility. That's how and why the North Carolina Fund got created. It succeeded even in its stated goal of doing its transitional job and going out of business. My guess is there is consensus of enough farsighted and/or scared people in our society now to let philanthropy operate much more freely in setting a different agenda in a different world. But I would also say that there are going to be some real confrontations. We can't minimize the risks. Both I and the authors may be led by our biases to do so.

Waldemar Nielsen: It seems to me that Douglas and Wildavsky are trying to put a focus on what they consider to be one important and somewhat neglected emphasis in foundation activity. The specific, the central question they pose is this: Has there in fact been a tendency for foundations to neglect or draw back from trying to do constructive appraisals and examinations of government programs? We have to rely so much on government to deal with so many of the problems in our national life, and so many 'of these government programs are in fact failing, that such foundation activity is a very important need, whether we're talking about unemployment in the ghettos, inflation, or many other things. I think they have asked an extremely important question, and my answer is, yes, this is an important and somewhat neglected role or function of philanthropy.

B.J. Stiles: The paper, and some of our reactions, lumps together some very dissimilar institutions and experiences and fails to develop adequate or helpful frames through which to view these concerns. Both foundations and the government are painted indiscriminately. We're attacking and defending behaviors and patterns here which are not monolithic. I'm uncomfortable with some of the equations we're making.

To talk about HEW and its relationship to health problems is not comparable to talking about the National Science Foundation and its relationship to scientific research and knowledge. We should ferret out such distinctions and try to sharpen our understanding and description of these conflicts and agreements—those within private philanthropy as well as those between private philanthropy and government.

For example, the paper focuses on what are termed the "knowledgeable foundations." I recognize the utility of that shorthand jargon, but it jars my understanding of what constitutes knowledge. Action and experience, as well as basic research, are part of the knowledge-shaping process, and we harm the accuracy as well as the utility of this conversation if we settle for either narrow or traditional perspectives. I have much sympathy for Paul Ylvisaker's comments in this regard.

My second concern is with the tendency to focus on size as the preeminent barometer of impact when looking at both foundations and government. Bigness has to be acknowledged, but other criteria merit attention. As a Southerner, active in the fifties and sixties in struggles to alter the ethnocentrism of my region, culture, and generation, I and many of my contemporaries benefited from the support of foundations that would not likely be termed "knowledgeable"—at least in the context of this paper—and certainly weren't big. Several of these smaller foundations played a critical role at a strategic time by supporting individuals and organizations which challenged the status quo. These were not easy or popular commitments.

I cite these examples because I think they represent opportunities which are unlikely to attract early support from larger or corporate foundations, or the government. Risk taking need not be tied to size, as evidenced in John Knowles's reminder of the courage, audacity, and vision required to sustain the Rockefeller Foundation's commitment to work on problems of population, nutrition, and food scarcity. But the imagery of risk taking is not the critical problem which faces most of society's larger institutions.

For the major foundations, and much of government, the problems are very similar: There are more requests and expectations involving maintenance than there are proposals to undertake venturing or pioneering work. We in NEH deal with many of the same organizations that the larger foundations deal with. And, as the impact of inflation gets tougher and you give more terminal grants, the major consortia of intellectuals, academicians, and scholarly organizations come to the government simply because it's the only other source. The Douglas-Wildavsky paper presumes that there is an intent in government to control or influence major policies in these fields. I don't see either the intent or the practice. I do see a number of organizations coming to the government because there are no other likely sources for such major support.

Judging those needs and requests gets tougher and tougher as the needs and expectations rise. Therefore, I think it's inevitable that we in government have to be conversant with the leadership in private and corporate philanthropy. We have to learn from each other's mistakes. I think it's inevitable that we may feed off each other's biases, and therefore the cautions expressed by Paul Ylvisaker must be attended to. I don't see much difference between government and foundations on this point. I'm not sure that foundations are any more or any less independent than major universities, or national associations of scholars, or public-supported agencies.

Finally, the problems we are talking about are not terribly different from those associated with the federal budget. Although many people would like to believe that a shift in an administration or change in the Presidency will lead to immediate shifts in government spending, that isn't the way it works. Over three fourths of the federal budget is mandated, and only Congress can affect that. About 20 percent more is locked in for two to three years, and that leaves only a modest portion available for any short-term shifts in priorities.

I liked Paul Ylvisaker's suggestion that those in foundations should engage in a great independent dialogue with the mass of the people in all its heterogeneity. I would have some doubts, however, as to whether foundations really had a sufficiently broad constituency, a sufficiently broad range of contacts, to conduct this sort of dialogue. I agree that *that* type of dialogue does not take place, but I certainly haven't gotten the impression from what I've seen so far that American foundations are sufficiently populist for that purpose.

James Douglas: Perhaps my being British is a semantic problem here. Someone once said that we had everything in common with the Americans except the language, and I see that we've got caught on that one. My understanding is that the world "malaise" does not mean the same thing as "malady." Malaise means to me, literally, "sense of unease, of anxiety, of worry," very much what Dr. Knowles himself describes.

I started studying this area from scratch. There are few foundations in England of any size, and it is a much less important sector of the community. I came from a background in politics and with the idea that you seem to be in the ideal world. You are not subject to the main constraint which has been the bane of my life for the last 25 years and that is, How on earth do you sell this to the electorate? Nor are you subject to the constraint that affects my friends in business: How do you make a profit on it?

Yet, as I talked to people from foundations, they seemed uneasy and uncertain about their role. What we were trying to do in our paper was to fly a kite about one possible role which they might have. We end up by suggesting it as a basis from which to start the sort of discussion which has emerged around this table.

We fastened on a relatively small range of large foundations. I'm very well aware that there is a wider universe of American foundations which we really totally ignored and have learned nothing about as yet. I accept that as a perfectly valid charge.

I think it was Mr. Nielsen who said that government has

mucked up a lot of its new enterprises by overreaching. This is very close to what we suggested foundations ought to be looking into. Historically, it seems to me, foundations started by looking at the failures of the liberal capitalist system in the economy. Society on both sides of the Atlantic has moved away from a situation where the main power lies in the commercial sector to one where there's increasing power in the state, and this suggests we should be looking in a different direction to see when the main dangers may arise.

John Knowles: I think you both exemplify the views of the public at large. You clearly have not researched what we are in fact doing. I have to make that point because in fact we are now and have been doing exactly what you want us to do. You in fact did not analyze us, either through asking us or reading our reports or reviewing with us our inner workings as to where we stand on these matters. In that way, you are no different from most of our critics, who simply don't know what the hell they are talking about and are too lazy to find out.

Paul Ylvisaker: There's one part of the paper that I don't think we ought to miss. As I recall the phrase somewhere, one of the recommendations is to study philanthropy as a critical analytical force. I've been struck by the fact that in different universities we've got schools of business, schools of government, but no schools of the third sector. We've got case studies in business, case studies in government, but no case studies in philanthropy except as they begin to emerge with some resistance. I find the students I deal with increasingly interested in the third sector, and in the philanthropic process.

There is a creative restiveness inside a foundation, staff debates that are rich dialogues, far richer than we know because they are not publicized. I would like to see more of that exposed and understood. It doesn't have to be through popular writing so much because that tends to be too simplistic. But the kind of analytical interest that I've seen in the universities should be encouraged. It's beginning to emerge at such places as Yale and its school of public management.

George Bonham: I think that one of the difficulties of scholars doing such research and evaluation is that it would be very difficult for most scholars to be totally honest because more and more of them do depend in part on the goodwill of foundations.

Paul Ylvisaker: Point well taken—but there is still some honesty even among grantees.

Fred Hechinger: I don't have any problem with the call for the foundation to serve as an analytic monitor of what other sectors, particularly the government, do. But I would want to be very cautious not to overplay that role, because it seems to me that we're already an overanalyzed society. We have infinite varieties of evaluation and checks and rechecks on everything, and I would hate to have the foundations become overly concerned with that aspect of their function and move away from what in the end really does count, which is taking action and not doing analyses.

I would not want the foundations to become too top-heavy in their concern with finding out what others are doing that isn't working without also concentrating on what they can do to bring about action.

Aaron Wildavsky: I'm a little fearful from this morning's discussion that we will not in fact generate an appropriate and self-critical response, but rather a largely self-satisfied one. There is a difference, as we all know, between public and private knowledge, and I'm sure that there is a vast lode among operating executives and board members in the foundation field that has not reached its way into print in any form. If it is indeed true that you are doing what is being asked in numerous ways (and this has remained for some strange reason undiscovered), then you might look to why this is so. Certainly the corrective mechanisms are there.

Our paper is written to try to raise certain fundamental questions. It is true, as has been hinted here more than once, that we are a bunch of upstarts. Jim and I used to call ourselves the new boys. How new we hardly realized at the time. But simply saying that we've got it wrong in a general way is insufficient. Both of us would be very happy to get chapter and verse of how we got it wrong.

I have for a long time been an admirer, I hope a practitioner, and defender of what is called pluralist doctrines. But I have

become (after some acquaintance with foundations) more recep-
tive to the more radical critics of pluralism, when you find it being
used simply to cast aside inquiries, simply palming off somebody
who says, "Well, this or that might possibly be wrong, or
something seriously different should be considered," with the answer that we do an awful lot of that sort of thing, a little bit here
and there. I would turn the matter around and say that it's not sur-
prising that it is the large foundations with representative boards
that do representative things. I have heard some foundations that
have very large discussions of what they should do and, given the
boards that they have and the people that they have, they end up
quite often discovering that what they're doing is pretty much the
range of agreement as to what they ought to be doing.

From my point of view, the way to think about this is that if indeed foundations are doing representative things, then why should
they be preferred to representative governments? The logic of that
would be to suggest that they might well be merged with existing
political institutions which would give government slightly more
money because there would then be no differentiating characteristic between them and other representative institutions except that
these representative ones have a claim to be genuinely representative, a claim that no foundation could actually make. To put it
another way, if in fact it were true that foundations can't be controversial beyond a certain degree, then the response to that might
well be why not make them genuinely democratic—that is, distri-
bute their budget exactly the way the government budget is being
distributed. That, I think, has to be faced up to.

Much of what has been said here I would classify under the Lov-
ing Embrace doctrine. I do not doubt for one moment that foundations are useful to society and to government because they do
some things that government isn't doing—a little earlier than government is doing them, and a little differently than government is
doing them. People in the government know people in foundations and find that some of the foundations can do some things
that government has difficulty in doing with not quite so many
restrictions. You can then get an additional inquiry going. But
when I follow that rationale out to some sort of conclusion, it is
basically that foundations will be taken over in a fundamental
sense, taken over by government in a way that was never possible
before. It was never possible to imagine them being taken over by

business because businessmen basically care about two things: that you have a good reputation and you shouldn't kick the hell out of them. If you meet these two very simple criteria, you'll generally be all right, especially after you get rid of the founders and the lying dies out and they care about other things.

But government has so many people who care about what foundations do. We saw in this paper a situation in which foundations would become a useful adjunct of government, more and more, but that this did not reach fundamental questions.

Now I suppose the only one I fundamentally disagree with here, because I agree with many of the things that have been said, is Mr. Hechinger. As I hear him, all we really need is to do more of one kind and another and government should do more—everybody should do more and what we need basically in our society is more collective activity.

That certainly is not my view. It certainly is a view that ought to be challenged. So let me then just do something that isn't done in the paper, which is to talk about the rise of government and then come back to the comments that have been made here.

I think there is very serious doubt among many people as to the benefits of large government. Almost everywhere I travel in the world (not only in the USA—recently in Israel) I talk to members of the Labor Party who have just finished basically constructing all the aspects that you might think of as a welfare state. Publicly they love it. Privately they have very severe doubts. And there has to be doubt not only because it hasn't brought happiness but because they begin to see the interconnectedness of everything. They begin to see the range of unanticipated consequences. They begin to see the enormous built-in rigidities and wonder whether these are so much superior to what they displaced. They understand their own behavior and begin to see that, if government is the only game in town worth playing, then you'll never get anybody to resign, that resignations are few and far between, that the idea you're going to throw out Prime Minister Begin is ludicrous, because if people in a certain age group don't get to serve in government, they've lost almost all of the opportunity anybody in that society has had to do something significant.

Putting it another way, take the United States. In 1960 we spent approximately 20 percent of the federal budget on social welfare, broadly conceived, and 45 percent on defense. Today it's exactly the reverse. We're spending relatively and absolutely an enormous amount more on social welfare. What you can learn from this is that government can and does over a period of years change its priorities radically. This is the great reorientation in our perverted priorities that everybody was asking for in the sixties. Then why are we unhappy? We're unhappy because the consequences for individual behavior, for health habits, for recidivism rates, for reading scores, for whatever, turn out either not to be in our control or actually in some sense to have worsened. It is not so different after all from the green revolution, to refer to John Knowles's example of miracle rice and miracle wheat, which as we know has increased the demand for capital, which improves the position of peasant entrepreneurs, which creates and strengthens the middle class, and which has all sorts of consequences apart from its marvelous technological character. These are consequences that everybody is not certain are desirable with an expanding population, with unemployment, and all of the rest.

It is in this context that we find ourselves now. Our ability to measure failure is so much greater than our capacity to cause success that the vast reorientation of priorities on the macropolicy level is not followed by improved behavior at the micropolicy level. You have vast disappointments. The more government does, the more apparently it is criticized.

Therefore, instead of simply having the old-line argument on the Left and Right, where a radical foundation is one that says the government is no good, and the customary one says that government is good, one might consider a much more fundamental challenge, which is to ask questions that have hardly been touched: What is government good for and what isn't it good for? Are there inherent limitations for this or that activity? Maybe government should be doing a lot more in certain areas and a lot less in others. Questions such as these are not being asked. I've tried to find discussions of government failures or limitations on government. I've so far run across one paper that has not yet been published and that I fear only economists will understand—if even they do. So that the kind of query that could be raised about these matters has hardly been raised at all, even though I'm aware that foundations are critical of government, that they touch on many sorts of evaluations here and there, but not of a more fundamental kind.

The doctrines of pluralism that have sustained foundations in the past do not appear to me to be viable any longer. For one thing, the amount of money they have is sufficiently smaller, in real terms, so that you cannot invest in sufficient diversity to make good on the premise of pluralism. For another thing, the role of government has become so massive that doing a little bit here and there just absolutely pales. We have said in this paper that foundations have in some sense become both more vulnerable and visible: In absolute terms they are doing more, but their relative contribution has become much smaller. It is thus incumbent on foundation people to ask questions like these: Should they really be adjuncts of business and serve a commercial purpose? Is just doing things a little bit different or earlier or slightly better or sometimes worse than government work for a grown person?

In talking to a few foundation people, and certainly in reading widely in the literature, we find very little discussion of issues of this kind. Should we take a more fundamental role, for instance, in doing what may be necessary to maintain political competition in this country? We have a party system that's almost moribund. Three quarters of the state legislatures are Democratic, and it's very difficult to imagine that in any election the Democratic character of Congress will be changed. This must have very powerful implications for the kind of society and the kind of criticism we are going to have.

I suppose you could just interpret our paper in sum by saying that there need to be analyses of a wholly changed era, where cultural mores have undergone significant change, where the relation of the state to the individual has undergone significant change, where size of government affects practically everything. It shouldn't be unexpected that the role of foundations should also be debated. I agree with Mr. Bundy that the exposed political position of foundations is vastly overestimated and this is one thing we thought we tried to say in the paper. We think that they are not nearly so exposed as they think. If that were not our view, we would find it difficult to recommend even more fundamental queries on their part because that would obviously then lead to their extinction. It has been my personal experience, and the experience of some people that I have talked to, that within many foundations the lessons of 1969 and thereafter are quite different in character from the one that has been suggested here. That lesson has been widel ·nterpreted to suggest that foundations ought not to get into certain things at all. Some have simply learned to accommodate themselves and don't try to do this with that.

Often the IRS is summoned up as a bogey man, as if it's going to drop from the sky. I tell you that Chicken Little lives in American foundations.

McGeorge Bundy: It seems to me that's just what's wrong with the paper: that it's very indiscriminate. I would have gladly circulated large quantities of materials I would have thought were accessible, including my own efforts to review these matters. Some four years ago, I wrote a paper called *Public Policy and Private Foundations*, which I'll be glad to share with you.

Fred Hechinger: You cite the problems of the American party system. I completely agree that there is much room for critical discussion of why the party system is in the state you suggest. And I assume that political scientists at major universities do that, or if they're not doing that, ought to be. I don't know that they need specifically to be told by foundations to do this or even be supported by foundations in their efforts. I assume this is part of their normal work.

Aaron Wildavsky: I have no doubt that this question is in fact being studied as much as anybody can understand it, which is certainly very little. But the question of criticism within the system— that is to say, given the growth of large government and the inevitable clientelism that accompanies it, with the vastly larger stakes that employees of government and beneficiaries have in what goes on—that is very little discussed.

McGeorge Bundy: What specifically is missing? That's what I don't understand. I quite understand what I would call your large-scale point that there is a shortage of Schumpeterian analysis of the current condition of the political economy. I think that's right. Schumpeters are rare, and if our foundation or any other could find one it would be very well advised to back him. But what I don't understand is your assertion that there is missing criticism of the middle level of government performance. My desk is loaded with it.

Aaron Wildavsky: In a way, that is what I object to because to do a bit of everything is a cop-out. I don't expect foundations to fill in everything. But I think, from the foundation viewpoint, the question of balance between the public and private economies should assume greater importance. If government or private industry grows too powerful—and I focus on government only because in the present era it does not appear that business is in too great a danger of growing too powerful (I could change my mind in different historical circumstances)—then that will have a vast impact on the role of independent foundations. I think the possibility of foundations being not only a third sector, but consciously assuming a position of a third force interested in the relation between the other two, has not been touched at all.

McGeorge Bundy: What I can't get at is why you think foundations are reluctant to support these kinds of proposals. I don't mean to particularize, but the example is useful, I think: Yesterday, we spent an hour and a half listening to Charles Lindblom talk about his next book, which relates precisely to these questions—the relationship between what he calls professional social inquiry and government. Does it work, and is social science research productive? You make an assumption that we are hostile to this kind of inquiry, which I believe to be unfounded.

James Douglas: I don't think we assume hostility. In fact, I have enormous admiration for the American foundation. You've got to live in a country where there aren't any foundations to realize what an enormous flexibility is inherent in a large private sector that's devoted to public good.

Waldemar Nielsen: What you have to understand as a Britisher, I think, is that one of the greatest talents of American foundations is to detect hostility in even the most dispassionate and constructive efforts to discuss and analyze foundation performance.

Aaron Wildavsky: Let me try to put it more precisely. I would say that there is a reluctance among foundations to believe that they don't have an acceptable rationale for their role, and that therefore they might sponsor research of one kind or another. But the question of living it, of taking seriously the question of devising a rationale by which they can live, is quite another thing.

John Knowles: You're not being clear. One of the problems we have here quite frankly is that the level of scholarship is building up a pile of straw men and self-fulfilling prophecies. Can we be specific?

Fred Hechinger: Let me give some examples, which are closer to what you were suggesting in terms of government. Ford's support of Jencks or Carnegie's of Keniston, both of whom I think are wrongheaded, is what you are talking about. I happen to disagree with the thrust of their recommendations. But that's irrelevant. They are precisely the kind of things you suggest foundations are not doing.

Aaron Wildavsky: I think the tendency I detect here to make critics into disappointed seekers after largesse is a mistake.

McGeorge Bundy: No, I'm not suggesting that at all. I'm suggesting a quite different point, which is that I do think it is true that for very large foundations, and certainly for the one that is the largest, plurality is virtue. For us in the Ford Foundation to focus only on the particular question you raise, Is government getting too big and falling over itself and squashing the values of society under its own mindless mass? would seem to me to be a curious distortion of the opportunities and the challenges that come in.

If it were ignored or regarded with hostility, that would be an extremely legitimate and serious reason for criticism. But I'm trying to find out which of the two you are asserting.

Paul Ylvisaker: I don't want to blunt the eruption of feeling here, but let me ask this: The ground rules of society are what philanthropy now could productively be concerned with. The one ground rule that I'm surprised you didn't talk about in your paper —as a matter of fact, you glided over it in such a way as to make me fearful—was your acceptance that government can regulate. You don't state the terms. You accepted 1969 without getting into the relationship between philanthropy and the First Amendment. It isn't that I'm absolutely certain that you ought to come out, as Justice Harry Blackmun once did, and say, "This is a categorical right; you shall not take it away."

But philanthropy has accepted through the tax exemption limitation on its First Amendment rights. If it's going to play the role
you're describing of a free agent in society and criticize whatever,
doesn't it need more protection than it has under the Tax Act, the
implications of exemption, and so on? Why is that missing in the
discussion? I've never seen a major foundation talking about this.

John Knowles: Now this is a very key point. If we really do our
jobs and tell government where to head in, then we're going to be
before the House Ways and Means Committee and the Senate
Ways and Means Committee and they'll get the hell rid of us. Government does not like these so-called isolated islands of power sit-
ting here throwing spit balls at them. So I'm with you. I'd like to
hear a little more of that while they exhort us to go after government. Ultimately, government, representing the people, I suspect,
decides what is going to happen to us. Fine—that's democracy—
but central power has grown and it swats gadflies and hell raisers
with more and more impunity.

Paul Ylvisaker: There should be a Magna Charta for philanthropy, and it should address specifically that question.

Waldemar Nielsen: My idea on this is that just as some people in
philanthropy underestimated the political vulnerability of foundations in 1969, so some of them may be overestimating their invul-
nerability today. I think that one aspect of your question, Paul, is
obviously legal, constitutional. But another aspect of it is obviously political and attitudinal. We know that under the pressures of
what we've perceived as international threats in the postwar period, government intrusions upon constitutional liberties became a
standard practice. You mustn't forget that Mr. Alexander of the
IRS testified—I think it was just a year and a half ago—that the
IRS for 20 years maintained computerized dossiers on 465,000
Americans, and in his words, principally blacks, liberals, and an-
tiwar advocates. He also said that the maintenance of these dossiers had nothing to do "with the enforcement of the tax laws."

Looking to the future, it may be that we are entering another
period of severe international tension. It could be that the
American people are going to respond in a self-protective way,

and that governmental capacity and permission to intrude on these rights will increase again.

I would associate myself entirely with John's counsel of prudence here, particularly on the part of the big foundations. I think they do have to make their own calculation of public tolerance, so to speak, if they try to get into the business of being public scourge or public goad or public critic. Both for philosophical and very practical reasons, a diversity of program emphases is their sound course.

On the other hand, I would agree with Morris Abram—let me just quote a sentence of his which I encountered this morning. Speaking of the role of a foundation like the Field Foundation, of which he is chairman (that is a very small foundation relative to those represented at this table), he says, "I think there is a duty upon the foundation to be a public goad if not a scourge—an instrument of criticism and great affliction. Among the targets to be criticized are all instruments possessing power so great as to tend to insulate them from examination and review."

Personally, I think that for small foundations that may be a perfectly appropriate definition of their function, if that's what they choose to do. But I do not think that it would be a prudent and, over the long run, a productive or even tolerable definition of exclusive function for one of the major foundations in our country. Even if one accepts the validity of what I understood to be the criticism of the Douglas-Wildavsky paper, for big foundations there are definite limits and balances and considerations of prudence. They have to observe them if they intend to continue to carry on their useful work over the longer run.

McGeorge Bundy: There's a useful point of difference to be noted here that is treated only glancingly in the paper, and that is the difference between the foundation as grant maker and the foundation as operator. A particular recommendation in the paper, and it's one that I would have a lot of sympathy with for a relatively small foundation, is that a foundation should devote itself to a particular selective major problem and itself be the site of research and analysis and criticism on that major problem. That's an excellent choice, but it's not the only way to operate. Most of the third sector in the United States, educational as well as other nonprofits, regard foundations, and especially large foundations, as grant makers. And once you start making grants, you have an entirely different set of questions you have to ask about other people's ideas, other people's priorities, and other people's skills: And I think that distinction is worth bearing in mind.

George Bonham: Let me quickly return to Paul's reference to the constitutional protection under the First Amendment, which I think you argue perhaps inadequately in terms of the kind of political protection that foundations need. Is that what you think?

Paul Ylvisaker: The extent and limitations of the rights of expression of the third sector have never been explicitly argued out.

McGeorge Bundy: The puzzle is, Does the tax exemption limit the right to political activity? And my guess is that it always will be a puzzle.

George Bonham: And, conversely, you constantly have a threat of tax exemption withdrawal.

McGeorge Bundy: You always have the option of being taxed.

Paul Ylvisaker: If the third sector is to serve increasingly as an independent force in America, I think we ought to be quite explicit about its rights. If I'm a journalist, I can do research on any subject without any controls whatsoever (except for self-imposed restraints and the laws of libel). But academic researchers are facing an accumulation of regulatory processes—witness the controls on research on human subjects, National Institutes of Health guidelines on DNA research, etc. In that sense, the rights of free speech and inquiry are being circumscribed by the regulatory process. I'm torn between the recognition that such controls are necessary and an insistence on free inquiry.

Maybe prudence should be the answer here, a kind of a pragmatic common law that develops common sense constraints by emerging common law. But I haven't seen a good, explicit discussion of the basic issues involved. The academic community is beginning to cry halt. But the issue needs more than a defensive yelp —it needs a systematic dialogue.

George Bonham: I don't quite understand your point, Paul. Is adjusting the tax status of Harvard at stake for expressing views that are contrary to public pleasure? I think that threat is essentially what you're citing as opposed to that of a newspaper writer.

Paul Ylvisaker: No, not necessarily. I'm just saying that the third sector is being differentiated in an ad hoc way. Some controls are developing, some are needed, some are abhorrent. But that overriding concern for an independent third sector and its constitutional rights just hasn't been seriously discussed.

Waldemar Nielsen: This should be broader than foundations if it's going to be dealt with at all, in my opinion. Because almost all kinds of nonprofit institutions, apart from the strictly sacramental aspects of church activity and perhaps certain social action movements, are now involved with government, both as recipients of government funding and also as objects of government regulation, not special objects but objects along with other institutions of our country.

This is a new phenomenon. It results in a greater degree of conformity, a restriction upon their freedom of speech, and perhaps more often self-imposed or anticipatory than externally placed on them, but nonetheless real.

In the coming decade we could very well find ourselves again in a new situation of international tension, or internal tension, because of terrorism or other things, and that circumstance, plus their growing dependence on government money, could result in a double vulnerability for nonprofit institutions. So the time is here for all these marvelously quarrelsome and diverse elements of the third sector to try for once to compose their differences, at least in this particular area of common concern, and assert and insist upon certain conditions of freedom. If they were to try to do that, they could in toto enlist very considerable ranks of constituencies. They might therefore be able to protect themselves by that kind of common awareness and common effort. Foundations as such are almost the weakest and most vulnerable elements of the whole situation because they are unloved for their wealth and their origins, and they have no constituency.

Landrum Bolling: I think what Wally has just said touches on one of the things that I had hoped for in this paper but didn't find: That is a way of relating the foundation community to the broader third sector in general. And not only the First Amendment issue has to be seen in that broad context. You simply cannot defend the turf of foundations alone. Our identity has to be linked with that of the others in this broad third sector.

I wanted to speak also to the question of the relationship between government and foundations and the necessity to study that relationship more carefully. I don't think that we ought to see that relationship always just in terms of confrontation or conflict or disagreement. One of my great fears about this relationship is that the foundations are increasingly co-opted by government so that we become only very, very inconspicuous tails to the government kite. The authors of this paper tried to address that in some way, but I thought there was a rather considerable lack of specificity about those relationships and what might be done about them.

One of the things that appalls me is the way in which federal policy with regard to the support of the arts has proceeded with the most casual indifference to the effect that these policies and actions of government have upon private philanthropy in relation to the arts. Many foundations around the country are finding themselves driven into a corner where they are really going to be bad boys in their communities if they don't fork up the required matching money for what the Endowment has decided should be done.

George Bonham: I fear that foundations, both private and public, are at times wholly insensitive to the mischief that matching challenge grants may bring. That option should first be discussed with the grantee, as to whether it really serves the grantee's best interests. I can only tell you that the government's present support formula for public television calls for one federal dollar for every $2.25 collected by the stations themselves. Have you any idea what pressures are then built up to solicit viewers and corporate sponsors in playing such matching games?

John Knowles: You're looking at somebody who's been resentful about that ever since I got here. I've spent the first six years arguing with Nancy Hanks of the National Endowment for the Arts over who was going to do what. Every idea we developed, they couldn't match. Everything they had, we were expected to match, which we did not. But the pressure from constituencies is considerable. In some instances this isn't all bad by any matter of means; but the quaint notion that the foundations would match the $120 million or so from the humanities and arts endowments has in fact not worked at all. The heat is on us to use our very limited resources to help them out in various parts of the country. Our best role is to lead *their* big money into the support of new areas of creativity that we have developed with our meager but much more flexible money.

Fred Hechinger: If the foundations are to be at all concerned about government performance and government policy, I would be very uneasy if they didn't consider the corporate sector as well. I say this in spite of all the ideological rhetoric from the Right about the danger of big government. I don't have any question that the power of the corporations, particularly in the international field, is far greater than even that of the government. It is enormous in terms of determining what the government can and cannot do. An awful lot of actions that the government might want to take are not taken, whether in the field of energy or in the area of political issues, because of the power of corporations. I'm not suggesting that we ought to look at that sector as a villainous force. But it's unrealistic to omit that whole sector from the concern of the foundations, particularly if we concentrate that heavily on the foundations' critical relationship with government. If we did this it would simply have the effect of making the ignored sector even more powerful in the shaping of the kind of policies—social, economic, and otherwise—that we ought to be concerned about.

George Bonham: I think that's an interesting point. We talked earlier about the fact that, for constitutional reasons, foundations are rather beholden to government. Is it not also fair to say that, with few exceptions, foundations, the large representative foundations, are very much beholden to business?

Waldemar Nielsen: I would quite agree with Fred's view. I would not only include corporations but also other major institutions of national life, such as trade unions, churches, and the universities. Conceptually, one of the useful and rather unique roles that foundations can play—not because they are utterly free of bias or the influence of their own associations but because after all they have their own money and over time do develop a greater degree of independence of their origins—is that they can seek to appraise objectively, criticize where they feel it's necessary, and put forward constructive recommendations to the various major institutional elements of our kind of a pluralistic democracy. And that includes government. Quantitatively, government is bigger than any of them, but agriculture and labor and so on all represent in some way that same essential opportunity. I would hope that different foundations would find it interesting to address themselves to one or another or several of these possibilities as they see fit.

John Knowles: Generally speaking, business is even more anti-foundation than antigovernment. Pat Moynihan once wrote that the foundations and the private sector have sown the seeds of their own destruction because what they do is support universities where intellectuals (largely liberal, on Nixon's hate list) have steadily said that what we need is more government and bigger government, better government, more legislation, more spending and all will be well. So we've been feeding these intellectuals. We don't feed the conservative intellectuals and there aren't many to feed. We haven't even talked about the American Enterprise Institute, which claims its major difference with Brookings is that its scholars try to strengthen the private sector, whereas Brookings tries first to strengthen government.

Now, clearly, it's not that simple by any measure, but AEI has gone from a budget of $80,000 to $7 million, and they've got all kinds of interesting people. I think that business is goddamn mad at foundations and the universities right now. Clearly, businessmen don't understand foundations either, at least not the large ones.

So let's add another one. The government doesn't like us. If you think business people will stand up for us, I can promise you they won't. Many businessmen have the most distorted view of what we're up to, and it's not in their best interest, the way they see us.

That takes care of two potential supporters. Now comes the third. We at Rockefeller have 10,000 applicants a year. Five hundred of them we fund and they think we should have given them more. The other 9,500 feel absolutely rotten and dislike us for our stupidity and callous indifference. Both feel an ultimate hostility, which they can't express to us. Now I'm not paranoid. I sit here and smile and say this is reality. I can also say that there are many people from all walks of life and in many different countries who respect and value what the Rockefeller Foundation has done.

B. J. Stiles: You should sit in Washington with William Hewitt [chairman of the board of John Deere & Co.] and Robert Nisbet [professor of humanities at Columbia] on your board and then have the *New York Times* attack you because (a) you're over politicized, and (b) you're not giving enough money to New York City.

McGeorge Bundy: There is a risk here in making these sectors look like monoliths. I was trying to identify the businessmen who remain on our board of trustees. John's discussion didn't fit them very well. The government also is a fairly complex phenomenon. It's just not that simple. There is not a very large force with one single hostile weapon, which is the IRS, aimed at the foundations. It doesn't work that way.

The way the National Endowment for the Humanities operates —these are simple points but I think we are neglecting them—is different from the way the National Science Foundation operates, for lots of historical reasons. Yet they are much more alike than HEW, which Pat Moynihan now calls "The Thing." As Wally has pointed out, the third sector never has been a sector in its own self-consciousness. It doesn't operate that way.

Aaron Wildavsky: Do you think that it is necessary for foundations to change their rationales in view of the rise of large-scale government, and, if so, how?

McGeorge Bundy: I think so. But I also think, Aaron, that you're asking us to do something that we think we have been trying to do for 10 or 15 years.

John Knowles: I could give you 20 different examples where in fact we are working on sensitive issues. We just published a study on breeder reactors and nuclear energy. And I'll tell you quite frankly that some people on our board were very upset with this because it's in opposition to Mr. Carter's present policy. Now that gives us a problem at the level of our board and it could be a political problem, too.

McGeorge Bundy: An excellent example of diversity because, although I haven't read it yet, my people tell me that it's highly critical of work paid for by the Ford Foundation.

John Knowles: Then there is South Africa and southern Africa. We have retained Franklin Thomas, the ex-head of the Bedford Stuyvesant Corporation, a graduate of Columbia and its law school, to assess whether it would be valuable to this country at this juncture to form a national commission vis-à-vis the United States foreign policy toward South Africa.

Don't forget for one minute that in a democracy you've got lots of constituencies looking at us. If we decided rationally that we should get out of the population problem, I can tell you exactly what would happen: I'd go with it. If we tried to get out of the subject of minority groups, which we don't want to, I can tell you what would happen here too. Now, that's a given, but if we work with our board and go at it hard, we can still make substantial changes here, and we are still much more flexible than any other institution, public or private, that I know to this day.

Paul Ylvisaker: What I hear Wildavsky and Douglas saying is: Yes, we would admit the gradual, the continuous process of adjustment (and having been in philanthropy, I don't think any institution in society adjusts as rapidly and continuously to change as the major foundations). But what they're adding—and warning us of—is that we've come to a thermostatic point on the continuum of social change where suddenly life and its problems are qualitatively different. What Wildavsky is calling for, and I hear it, is an explicit recognition of a point in time where the critical function of philanthropy he's talking about needs reappraising and redirecting. Some of us here are saying they're crying "Wolf!" Frankly, I'm ready to listen, but I have thoughts about how to respond.

George Bonham: I think all of us are talking about a need to sustain some sensible power balance between our three sectors of social activity. A drastic imbalance cannot help but become a worrisome development. Some sensible balance is also vital from the viewpoint of those who are grant seekers. Clearly, the work of the Council on Learning as a social critic could not continue if we were solely dependent on government or solely dependent on corporate grants. We try to secure half of our operating funds from the general public. Another fourth comes from philanthropy, and the remaining fourth from government contracts. It is perhaps not the best system in the world, but it balances interests sufficiently so that I can sleep at night.

Waldemar Nielsen: Like a policeman's lot, the lot of the individual who presumes even to raise serious questions about philanthropy is usually not a very happy one. But I hope that, nonetheless, Aaron, you will persevere. In a way, this inhospitality to criticism is to the credit of philanthropy. Philanthropy is a vocation of commitment and passion, and there is a quality of righteousness and militancy among people in foundations just as there is among environmentalists. So that if you're going to try to talk about some of their problems and your ideas about their work, it will take some considerable courage and conviction on your part. I really admire the effort Douglas and Wildavsky have made.

So often, it seems to me, when we talk about philanthropy, we quite naturally focus our attention on the most complex, the most visible, and intellectually perhaps the most interesting category of philanthropy, the tiny group of big foundations. They are a very mixed bag, in terms of quality and caliber and perspectives and lots of other things, so that they do provide fine nourishment for a lively and lengthy discussion.

But, still, there is that far larger category of creative middle-sized foundations in the United States. And then there is that great multitude of rather amateurish or unstaffed but still well-meaning and useful small foundations. These different categories have different potentialities. They have different patterns of concentration in their work, and I would hope sometime that we could begin to give those middle-sized and smaller foundations as well as corporate foundations their due attention.

George Bonham: I want to get back to an important point, and particularly important I think for those in education. B.J. Stiles mentioned it first: That is the choices foundations have to make today on the issue of maintenance support versus risk taking.

McGeorge Bundy: I can speak to that very briefly because it was really the first large problem I had to deal with when I came to the Ford Foundation. In the days of its relatively much larger size, Ford had become an operational, quantitative force in a field like faculty salaries. But if you looked at the numbers and assumed that you would be interested in more than one institution, it simply became a mismatch. There is no way that the organized private foundation can be an important source for maintenance money for the field of higher education, or even for the once included field that I would perhaps choose out of my sense of relevance and need in the contemporary situation, the field of the major research university.

The numbers are off by zeroes. Therefore, the foundation that I work for has tried to devote its attention in this field to the puzzles and problems of other sources, of which the largest, for the research university, is now the federal government, wearing one hat or another. That is a very important area, as we have said in different ways around the table; if you can't find ways of reconciling the objective of freedom and the requirement of funding through taxes, you're in very serious trouble. I'm on the whole an optimist on this point, more optimistic than Wally Nielsen, I think. But the threat he describes certainly exists and to the degree that it becomes operational, it has to be fought.

Landrum Bolling: I don't frankly think we've fully dealt with the central question Douglas and Wildavsky put to us. As I heard it, I wrote it down in two forms: What is government good for? What is government not good for?

You've asked a very broad, sweeping question, the same kind that John Knowles's board has asked him about foundations: Do they have a reason to exist? Well, I think that, of course, government obviously has a reason to exist and will always exist. But I think as it is being raised here in your paper I'm not sure what foundations can do about it. But I'm sure that we do need to get a more honest kind of dialogue about the real function of government in modern society and the limitations of government. We have an awful lot of pious rhetoric one way or the other about that kind of question. We've been drowning in conservative rhetoric for years about the too great expansion of government and it so confused us that many people just reacted instinctively against any discussion of the question. But you've now got today, I think, an emerging shared concern. We've got to look at the whole question and the scale of government and what it is government can do and why is it that the government makes such monstrous failures of so many good things it tries to do? What are the problems here? That's a broad question, and it's so broad that I don't know how you can get your hands on it. But I think that issue ought to be addressed, and I don't think the foundations have addressed that.

Aaron Wildavsky: I agree entirely with what Mr. Bolling has said. But I have an addition to make. It would not be sufficient, from the point of view of understanding foundations, merely to say that they ought to study a very interesting issue of modern times. I'm sure they are in some ways studying it, and that would not call for any further comment.

What we were trying to suggest is that there is a connection between what government is and is not good for, and what future roles foundations might play. For a long time, early foundations were involved in dealing with the consequences of an industrial society and trying to ameliorate those consequences. Then in very large measure government stepped in to deal with these market imperfections and stepped in in a gigantic way.

The question is that if government is dealing with market imperfections, who is dealing with government imperfections? If we understood better the classes of inherent difficulties of government, then we might devise a possible rationale for different foundations, one rationale for every sort of inherent difficulty, and this would provide a beginning in trying to have a more satisfactory discussion of what the role of different types of foundations might be in the modern era.